The Gita
FOR CHILDREN

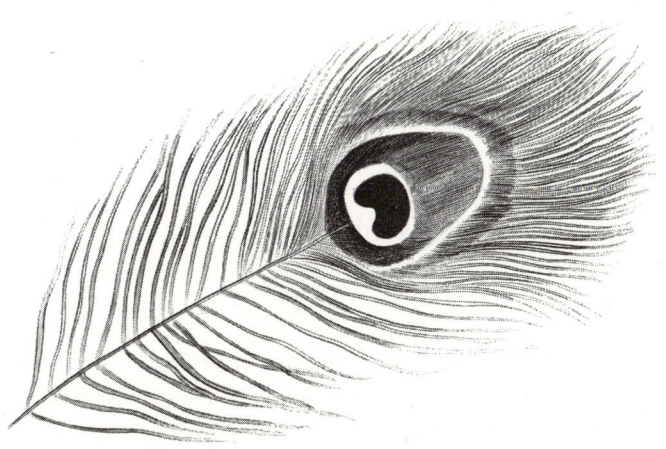

Bengaluru-based author, columnist and speaker, **Roopa Pai** is one of India's best known children's authors. Many of her books, which cover a wide range of topics including popular science, history, economics, medicine and sci-fi fantasy, are bestsellers, and are enjoyed as much by adults as by children. Her most popular book, the award-winning *The Gita For Children* has been translated into many Indian languages and is listed by Amazon India as one of the '100 Indian books to read in a lifetime'. Her TEDx talk 'Decoding the Gita: India's Book of Answers' has received close to two million views to date.

When she is not writing, Roopa can be found teaching short introductory courses on ancient Indian wisdom to both children and adults. This computer engineer also leads groups of children and young people on history and heritage walks across her city, as part of her work as director of *BangaloreWalks*, a company she co-founded.

Sayan Mukherjee is a multidisciplinary illustrator from Kolkata, India. His work includes paintings, book covers, animated frames and much loved children's picture books drawn using various mediums. Sayan is also a muralist and has created expansive feature-scapes across India. A passionate visual storyteller, he uses bold, vibrant colours to reimagine the world around him uniquely. You can know more about his work at www.sayanart.net.

The Gita
FOR CHILDREN

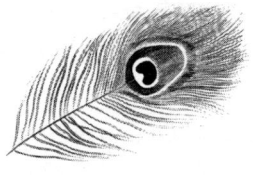

ROOPA PAI

Illustrations by Sayan Mukherjee

SWIFT PRESS

This paperback edition first published in Great Britain by Swift Press 2024
This edition first published in India by Hachette India 2022
Originally published in India by Hachette India 2015

3 5 7 9 8 6 4 2
Text copyright © Roopa Pai 2015, 2022
Illustrations copyright © Sayan Mukherjee 2022
Book design by Neelima P Aryan © 2022 Hachette India

The right of Roopa Pai to be identified as the Author of this Work has been asserted
in accordance with the Copyright, Designs and Patents Act 1988.
Page 31: Quote from *To Kill a Mockingbird* copyright © 1960 by Harper Lee,
Grand Central Publishing, Hachette Book Group USA
Page 34: Quote from *Cosmos* © 1980 by Carl Sagan, The Random House Publishing Group USA
Page 167–8: J. Robert Oppenheimer quote from atomicharchive.com
Page 169: Quote from Trinity Test, July 16, 1945, by eyewitness Brigadier General
Thomas F. Farrell from nuclearfiles.org copyright © Nuclear Age Peace Foundation 1998–2015

Typeset by Manmohan Kumar, New Delhi
Offset by Tetragon, London
Printed and bound in Great Britain by CPI Group (UK) Ltd, Croydon, CR0 4YY
A CIP catalogue record for this book is available from the British Library

We make every effort to make sure our products are safe for the purpose for which they are
intended. Our authorised representative in the EU for product safety is Easy Access System
Europe, Mustamäe tee 50, 10621 Tallinn, Estonia gpsr.requests@easproject.com

ISBN: 9781800751873
eISBN: 9781800751804

To the readers of this book...
Good luck finding the Krishna inside you – it won't be easy, but they say He is totally worth it

CONTENTS

So What's the Big Deal About the Bhagavad Gita?		xi
The Concatenation of Events That Led up to the Conversation		xix
Three Last Things (Promise!) Before We Plunge into the Conversation		xxx
1.	In Which the Stage Is Set for the Conversation	1
❧	In Which the Warrior Leaves the Field (At Least in Spirit)	13
2.	In Which Krishna Gives Arjuna a Stern Talking-to	25
❧	In Which Krishna Shares with Arjuna a Killer App for Contentment	39
3.	In Which Krishna More or Less Blocks Arjuna's Escape Route	46
❧	In Which Krishna Whips the Veil off Two Vile Villains	53
4.	In Which Krishna Reveals That He Is a Little Unusual	63
❧	In Which Arjuna Learns That Exercise Is a Valid Form of Worship	71
5	In Which Krishna Plugs Another Loophole	80
❧	In Which Krishna Describes the Happy Man – Again	86

6.	In Which Krishna Explains the Importance of Me-Time	89
◄◄	In Which Arjuna Learns That Just Trying to Be Good Can Win You Brownie Points in Your Next Life	97
7.	In Which Krishna Reveals That He Is Everywhere, and That Means Everywhere	104
◄◄	In Which He Who Is Beyond Classification Indulges in a Bit of Classifying	108
8.	In Which Krishna Reveals His Address and Provides a Roadmap for Getting There	116
9.	In Which Krishna Lets Arjuna in on the Great Secret	132
10.	In Which Arjuna Demands – and Gets – a Very Long List	141
11.	In Which Krishna Grants Arjuna's Wish – and Scares Him Silly	155
12.	In Which Krishna Gives Arjuna the True Devotion 101	170
13.	In Which Krishna Unravels a Deep and Complex Mystery	179
14.	In Which Krishna Provides Us with the Perfect Excuse for All Our Faults – 'It's Not Me, It's My Nature!'	191
15.	In Which the Conversation Takes an Unusual Turn – and Goes Topsy-turvy	203
16.	In Which Krishna Recommends That You Keep Your Demons Locked up – or Else	214

17.	In Which Krishna Holds Forth on a Variety of Subjects – in Triplicate	226
18.	In Which Arjuna Asks His Final Question	240
⋘	In Which Arjuna Learns to Tell Nectar from Poison	243
⋘	In Which Arjuna Learns That He Must Respond When Nature Calls	248
⋘	In Which Arjuna Receives a Precious and Unexpected Gift	250
⋘	In Which the Warrior Returns to the Field	253

Epilogue	262
A Note from the Author	272
Acknowledgements	276
Select Bibliography	279

So What's the Big Deal About the Bhagavad Gita?

You've heard of it, you've studied about it in History class, you've seen it take centre stage in court scenes in old Bollywood movies (Remember? When the actor standing in the witness box places their right hand on it and vows to tell the truth, the whole truth and nothing but the truth?). And you've often wondered why *so* many people get all solemn and dewy-eyed and worshipful about a book that, last time you checked, looked like the most difficult thing anyone could ever read. Well, let's find out, shall we? But first, let's figure out what you *really* know about the Bhagavad Gita (or the 'Gita' for short). All you have to do is tick the right option in the questions given below.

1. What is the Bhagavad Gita? Is it...
   a. A Sanskrit poem composed in India at least 2,500 years ago, the title of which literally means 'The Song of the Lord'?
   b. One of the holiest books of the Hindus?
   c. A small part of an Indian epic poem called the Mahabharata?
   d. A conversation between two friends called Krishna and Arjuna?

Roopa Pai

  e. A book of wisdom about how to live a good, righteous and happy life?

  f. All of the above?

Did you pick 'f'? 'All of the above'? Congratulations! That's the right answer!

And now that we have established that the Bhagavad Gita is part of the Mahabharata, we can proceed to the next logical question.

 2. What is the Mahabharata? Is it:

  a. The world's longest epic poem, composed about 2,500 years ago?

  b. One of India's two great Sanskrit epics (the other being the Ramayana)?

  c. The story of a Great War between two sets of cousins, the five Pandavas (aka the good guys) and the hundred Kauravas (aka the not-so-good guys)?

  d. A set of stories within stories, so intricately interwoven that very few people can claim to know all the stories and all the characters in it?

  e. The inspiration for innumerable books, a super-hit television series, and countless movies, plays and folk songs in every Indian language (and many foreign ones)?

  f. All of the above?

Of course you picked Option f again, and of course you're right. But now let's get into the details a little bit and see how you fare (Fun fact: There *isn't* an Option f anymore!).

3. The Mahabharata, which the Bhagavad Gita is part of, is made up of 18 Parvas, or books, each of which is further divided into chapters. How many chapters does the Gita itself have?

   a. 3
   b. 15
   c. 18
   d. 223

4. Just like the rest of the Mahabharata, the Gita is composed entirely in two-line verses, or couplets, called 'shlokas'. In all, the Mahabharata has more than 100,000 shlokas. How many of these make up the Gita?

   a. 22,300
   b. 700
   c. 43,455
   d. 1,278

5. Which Parva of the Mahabharata is the Gita a part of?

   a. The 6th
   b. The 16th
   c. The 1st
   d. The 18th

Okay, let's take a break here to tell you the right answers so far.

- The Bhagavad Gita has the same number of chapters as the Mahabharata has Parvas – 18.
- It has – surprise, surprise! – just 700 shlokas, less than 1 per cent of all the shlokas in the mother epic!

- It is part of the 6th Parva – yes, it makes an appearance quite early on in the story.

The question to ask, therefore, is this: How come a set of verses that is such a tiny part of India's great epic, is better known than the epic itself? What exactly makes the Bhagavad Gita so important and so revered? Only one way to find out – on to the next question!

6. We've already figured out that the Mahabharata is about a Great War, and the Gita is a conversation between two friends called Krishna and Arjuna. When does this conversation happen?
   a. In the days leading up to the Great War
   b. In the days after the Great War
   c. When the Great War is about to begin (like, at two minutes to start time)
   d. Bang in the middle of the fighting

7. What is this l-o-o-n-g 700-shloka conversation actually about?
   a. The glorious history of India
   b. Battle strategy
   c. Krishna telling a reluctant Arjuna why he should get up and fight the good fight
   d. Superstar archer Arjuna telling his charioteer Krishna why he should drive faster

Another quick break, to reveal the right answers to Questions 6 and 7:

- The Gita conversation started just a few minutes before the Great War began, and since it wasn't a short conversation, it almost certainly held everything up for a longish time. Yes, not the best timing for a long conversation, but there you go.

- It was mostly Krishna talking through the 700 verses, and he was essentially telling Arjuna to stop whining and start fighting the Great War.

Which, of course, leads us to the next set of questions. Except, this time, *you* are asking them.

8. You're kidding me, right? So one friend tells another friend to stop complaining and get going, and takes some 700 verses to say it, and *that* conversation becomes one of the greatest books of wisdom in the world? *Why*?

Ah, that's the real question, isn't it? The short answer is that it is because Krishna also told Arjuna *why* he should fight, even though it was going to be the hardest thing in the world for him to go to war against his closest family.

9. Even so, that conversation was between *them*, and it had its part to play in *their* story. Why is something that happened in a story, even the longest epic poem in the world, considered so wonderful, so wise and so important even today?

That's the interesting bit! You see, stories – especially old, old stories that still get told and read and discussed thousands of years after they were first written – are very often more than just stories. They are really parables, stories that contain within them hidden truths, lessons, morals and wisdom that we can all learn from. The Gita is one of the greatest conversations in the world to listen into, because what Krishna is telling Arjuna is really a message he is sending out to all of us, on how to live our lives in the most honest, best possible way.

The greatest stories are also allegories, which means that they work on many levels. On one level – the most obvious level – the story of the Mahabharata is the story of a Great War between two sets of cousins – one set noble, righteous, law-abiding and virtuous, the other corrupt, deceitful, crooked and unscrupulous. But on another level, the Mahabharata is about the battles that rage in our own minds and hearts each day, as we struggle to choose between what we know is right and good and *difficult*, and what we know is not-so-right, not-so-good and definitely way easier.

As humans – creatures that sit right on top of the evolutionary tree – we are special in many ways. But what makes us really unique is our ability to make choices – not only choices like pizza versus pasta or jeans versus shorts, but *moral* choices – right versus wrong, good versus bad, being nice versus being downright awful.

You would think that since we can tell so clearly who the 'good guys' are in our moral choices, it stands to reason that we should be backing them every time in our mind battles, but it is incredible just how often we let the bad guys win.

Each day, just like Arjuna on the battlefield of Kurukshetra, we make excuses for our weaknesses on the battlegrounds of our minds and hearts, and whine about the right choices being too scary, too hard, too lonely, or just not as much *fun*. We become confused about what the right thing to do is, and wish we could run away from the battle rather than face its consequences. But unlike Arjuna, we often shut out the Krishna who lives in all of us – the still, small voice of our conscience that tells us, loudly and clearly, what we really *ought* to be doing – and end up doing what is *convenient* rather than what is *right*. Over time, our inner Krishna, tired of being ignored, stops speaking altogether, leaving us confused and clueless about what the right answers are.

10. Okay. But where does the Gita come into all this? Does *it* have those answers?

Yup. Most of them, at any rate. Of course, it isn't the only book in the world that has these answers – the holy books of all other religions, great epics from all cultures, and many other books have them too – but this is *India's* blockbuster bestseller 'Book With The Answers'.

That's the big deal about the Gita. That is the reason why millions of Indians have gone back to it, again and again, over thousands of years, every time they are in distress or despair, every time they have been unsure about what the right thing to do is. And that is why you might want to try reading it for yourself.

Because, when you read the Gita, there is no escaping Krishna's gentle – but no-nonsense – diktat to his confused, nervous, heartsick friend, Arjuna, and through him, to all of us:

- Focus only on doing your duty; let the Universe take care of the consequences.
- Defend the good, destroy the bad.
- Be true to yourself.
- Never hesitate to fight the good fight with everything you've got, for as long as it takes.
- Talk to your closest friend – your inner voice – often and at length (yes, even if it takes 700 shlokas worth of time, and *especially* on the eve of a big battle) and listen to what he has to say.
- *That* is the secret to being happy. *That* is the secret of a good life. *That*, my beloved Arjuna, is the only way to live.

The Concatenation of Events That Led Up to the Conversation***

Once upon a time, many thousands of years ago, the king of the Bharatas ruled the land that we now know as India from his capital of Hastinapura (now placed about 100 km north–east of present-day Delhi, in Meerut district, Uttar Pradesh). This king had two sons. The older one, Dhritarashtra, should rightfully have been king after his father passed, but he was blind, which automatically disqualified him from kingship. Thus did the younger son, pale and sickly Pandu, who would never otherwise have had a chance to rule, get his lucky break and become king.

However, Pandu's happiness was short-lived. A venerable sage, whom he had unintentionally annoyed, laid on him a terrible curse – that he should never be able to have children. 'A king who cannot produce an heir is a completely pointless king,' thought Pandu sadly to himself. He gave up the throne and went off to the forest with his two wives, Kunti and Madri. Blind Dhritarashtra became the caretaker king, ruling the kingdom in his brother's name.

---

*Ooh, big word. But it just means a series of interconnected things – happenings within happenings, loops within loops.
**When we say 'the conversation', we mean of course the Conversation. Yeah, the one that Krishna and Arjuna had on that long-ago battlefield.

Overall, Dhritarashtra was well pleased with the way things had gone for him. As he saw it, he wasn't so much taking care of the kingdom for his brother as he was keeping it safe for the sons he was going to have. If things went to plan, that sickly, childless brother of his would pass on one day soon, and then no force on earth would be able to stop his sons from rightfully claiming the throne of Hastinapura for themselves.

***

In mythology, however, as in life, things have a way of not going to plan. Pandu would never be able to have children, but in a brilliant mythological loophole, his elder wife Kunti could!

How come? Well, Kunti had been taught a mantra by a venerable sage (not the same one who cursed her husband; there were hundreds of venerable sages wandering around the forests of India then). If she chanted the mantra with great devotion while focusing on any god of her choice, that god would come down to earth and give her a son. Yeah, that simple!

In the forest, Kunti chanted the mantra three times: first to Dharma (aka Yama, god of death and righteousness); then, a couple of years later, to Pavan (aka Vayu, the god of the wind); and then to Indra (lord of the heavens and master of the thunderbolt), and soon had three bonny boys to mother. She named them, respectively, Yudhishthira, Bhima and Arjuna.

It was natural that Kunti's co-wife, Madri, should get a little envious and a little despondent at the sight of Kunti's gambolling boys, and she did. Kunti, fully satisfied with the size of her brood, decided to be generous, and taught Madri the mantra too. Madri chanted the mantra to the Ashwini Twins (the gods of medicine) and got herself, at one shot, *two* lovely twin boys whom she named Nakula and Sahadeva. Together, the five sons of Pandu were called the Pandavas.

Too much happiness upsets the balance of the world, so tragedy, which was waiting in the wings, decided to play spoilsport. One beautiful spring day, when the birds chirped and butterflies fluttered and bees buzzed and flowers scented the air, Pandu died. Broken-hearted Madri flung herself on his funeral pyre, leaving Kunti to handle all the five boys single-handedly. It was all a bit much for Kunti, so she decided to head back to Hastinapura and throw herself and her sons at King Dhritarashtra's mercy.

***

Much had happened in Hastinapura since Pandu and his wives had left. Dhritarashtra had married a princess called Gandhari, and the two of them had had – hold your breath – one *hundred* sons and one beautiful daughter. (No, it hadn't been one hundred years since Pandu left. These hundred boys and their sister were all born almost at the same time – from hundred and one embryos that had been incubated in mud pots for several months until the babies were all grown and ready. Stuff like this happened all the time in ancient India.) The hundred boys were known as the Kauravas (or 'descendants of the Kuru clan', Kuru being their ancestor and one of the greatest kings of the land).

When his sister-in-law unexpectedly showed up at his doorstep years after she had left, and with five kids to boot, Dhritarashtra was more than a little dismayed. But he couldn't possibly turn away his dead brother's family, and what was another five brats in a household that already had a hundred and one? Or at least that's what the king told himself as he took them in. In the years to come, he would wonder, over and over, at the wisdom of that decision.

The 105 princes grew up together, learning the same lessons under the same teachers (Dhritarashtra was very fair that way). The trouble was, the five Pandavas consistently beat the heck out of their 100 cousins in every department. Among the 105 princes, Yudhishthira was the most honest and upright, Bhima was the strongest, Arjuna outclassed everyone else at archery, and Nakula and Sahadeva were the best horsemen on the field. Plus, all the Pandavas were just really nice young men – polite, gentle with those who served them, respectful of their elders, concerned about the people of their kingdom, and so on, so they were also loved by everyone. Predictably, the Kauravas, particularly the oldest, Duryodhana, a nasty piece of work who wanted to be the next king, hated their cousins' guts.

***

Years rolled by. Duryodhana, nervous that the elders would name Yudhishthira the next king, decided to do away with his five cousins. He pretended to have a change of heart and built them a brand-new palace in a distant town, where he invited them to stay the night. Very few people knew that the palace was built of highly inflammable lac and was going to be set on fire that night. Luckily, Yudhishthira was one of those very few people. When the dastardly deed was carried out, the Pandavas had already escaped through a secret tunnel that led to the forest.

Once there, they decided to stay put for a bit, and let Duryodhana believe they were dead. One day, they heard of an archery competition that the king of Panchala was hosting. The winner would get to marry the kingdom's princess, a dark-skinned beauty called Draupadi. The Pandavas decided to try their luck. Every other prince had tried and failed, when Arjuna, who was in disguise, walked over and easily hit the target — a spinning wooden bird on top of a tall post — squarely in the eye. Knowing that no one else in the kingdom had such unerring aim, Duryodhana realized who the archer really was, and was enraged that his plan had failed.

(An aside here: It was at this archery contest that the Pandavas first met their cousin, Krishna, the son of their mother's brother. They quickly became close friends.)

***

Meanwhile, the Pandavas returned joyfully to the forest, with Draupadi in tow, eager to share their happy news with their mum.

'Mother,' they cried, 'look what we have brought home today!' Kunti was busy saying her prayers. Without turning around, she responded in typical mumly fashion with, 'Whatever it is, my sweethearts, make sure you divide it equally among yourselves.'

Ouch. Now that mum had spoken, there was no going back. Draupadi became the wife of all five Pandavas, and there was nothing she or anyone else could do about it.

With everyone figuring out that the Pandavas were alive and well, there was intense pressure on Dhritarashtra to do the fair thing and give them half the kingdom. The king knew it was right and good that he should do so, but he got a little protective about his own eldest son, and gave the Pandavas the worst, most barren part of the kingdom to rule.

If there was one thing the Pandavas were not afraid of, it was hard work. They cleared the forests around their part of the kingdom, made the land fertile by digging irrigation channels and built themselves a fabulous, glittering new capital called Indraprastha (thought

to be located in the region of present-day New Delhi), which they ruled wisely and well.

Now of course that made Duryodhana even more jealous, and even more determined to destroy his cousins. With his sneaky uncle Shakuni (not his dad's brother – he was dead – but his mum's), he plotted to exploit Yudhishthira's one weakness, which was his love for a good game of dice, to bring about his downfall. (FYI, the game of dice does not involve much skill or strategy; it is a game of pure chance. There is no guaranteed way to win, except by cheating. Uncle Shakuni was Grandmaster of the Cheats.)

***

When Duryodhana invited Yudhishthira to a friendly game of dice, Yudhishthira could not resist the challenge. Through the course of the game, Yudhishthira kept losing, but did not stop playing, convinced that luck would turn his way soon (he did not suspect that the game was rigged). In each round, both sides had something big at stake – palaces, territories, their entire kingdoms. In each round, the Pandavas lost their stake. In the end, with nothing left to lose, Yudhishthira staked each of his four brothers as slaves, then their common wife, and finally himself – and lost them all.

King Dhritarashtra had had enough. He knew that his sons had won by cheating, and he decided it was time to step in. He insisted that the Pandavas be given their freedom and their kingdom back. Duryodhana was furious but could not disobey the king, and the Pandavas returned to Indraprastha, red-faced but free.

***

A few months later, Duryodhana was back in action, working on his dad to get him to invite the Pandavas back to another game of dice. This time, there would be just one game, and just one thing at stake. Whoever lost would have to go into exile in the forest for 13 years, with the added condition that they spend the thirteenth year in hiding. If they were 'found out' during that year, they would go right back into exile for another 13 years. In the end, Dhritarashtra succumbed and sent out the invitation.

Once again, Yudhishthira accepted. Once again, he played the game. And once again, he lost. The Pandavas, their wife, and their mother Kunti returned once again to the forest. Thirteen years later, after spending the last year in hiding successfully, they came back to claim their kingdom. But Duryodhana flatly refused. Noble Yudhishthira retracted his right to the kingdom, and instead asked for just five villages, one for each of the brothers. Duryodhana retorted that he would not even give them the amount of land that would fit on the tip of a needle.

There was only one honourable thing left for Yudhishthira to do, and he did it. He declared war against mighty Hastinapura.

***

Preparations on both sides began in full swing. To the elders in the family, it was clear that terrible destruction and devastation were at hand. Worried, they asked Krishna to do something. (Why Krishna? For one, he was a relative, not an outsider, and this was after all a family feud. Second, his word had great influence with the Pandavas. Third, he was of the same generation as the two sets of warring cousins, so he could talk to them more as a friend than as an elder, which meant he would be taken more seriously. Fourth, he was considered impartial, and respected by both the cousins and by the elders in the family. Fifth, he was himself a powerful king and therefore considered politically savvy.) Krishna got both sides together and tried to hold peace talks. But Duryodhana was thirsting for war and refused to negotiate. The talks failed. War became inevitable.

Both sides began frantic negotiations with other kings – neighbours, relatives, friends, friends of friends – trying to get them to fight on their side. More and more kings signed up, until the entire land had gotten embroiled in the family quarrel. The only one who hadn't picked a side was Krishna.

Both the Pandavas and the Kauravas wanted Krishna to fight on their side. Krishna made them an offer – one side could have his armies, one side himself. Except, he added, he wouldn't be doing any fighting himself. Instantly, Duryodhana called dibs on Krishna's armies. Secretly relieved, the Pandavas, who were always going for the other option, marched off happily, Krishna by their side.

And thus was the stage set for the Great War at Kurukshetra (which is the town that we still call Kurukshetra, located about 160 km north of Delhi, in Haryana). For 18 long days, the greatest warriors in the land faced each other and fought like lions, their roars resounding across the land. One by one, legendary heroes fell, never to rise again, drenching the dusty plains with their noble blood. One by one, entire clans were wiped off the face of the earth, denuding the land of good men, leaving only widows and wailing orphans behind.

But all that was still to come. Before that, before the first bow had twanged, sending the first arrow zinging through the charged air of Kurukshetra; before a single mace had been swung into an enemy skull, crushing it; before the first sword, glinting in the sun, had sliced through soft flesh, sending a warm red geyser spurting heavenwards; before the two armies had rushed at each other, murder on their minds and rage in their manic eyes; before all that, right at the very start of the Great War, was the Conversation.

Three Last Things (Promise!) Before We Plunge into the Conversation

More than 100,000 shlokas make up the Mahabharata. Who was the genius (and tireless!) poet who composed them, and how long did it take him?

Actually, what we know today as the Mahabharata started off as a much shorter story called *Jaya*, which was just about 24,000 shlokas long. These shlokas, which contain the core of the Mahabharata story, and include the Bhagavad Gita, are believed to have been composed by a sage called Vyasa (who is also a major character in the story!) over three years.

According to legend, Vyasa dictated these shlokas to Ganesha, who agreed to be the scribe and write them all down, on the condition that Vyasa did not pause anywhere in his dictation. Vyasa agreed, but on the counter-condition that Ganesha would write a shloka down only after he had understood it. The deal was sealed, but a pen could not be found. Impatient Ganesha

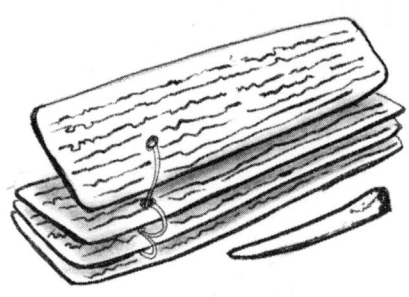

broke off one of his tusks (becoming Ekadanta, the one-tusked one) and used it to speedily record *Jaya* on palm leaves (our ancient version of papyrus).

But *Jaya* was never narrated to anyone by Vyasa himself. Legend has it that it was narrated by the sage Vaishampayana, a disciple of Vyasa, to King Janamejaya, the great-grandson of Arjuna the Pandava, just before he (the king) began a massive sacrifice to destroy every last snake and serpent in the world. [Janamejaya's dad, Parikshit, had died of snakebite, so the loving son had decided that, as far as revenge ratios went, a million (snake) lives to one (dad) life was about right.] This version of the epic, which included the conversation between Vaishampayana and Janamejaya, was called *Bharata*.

Many years later, and with several voluminous additions, *Jaya* was narrated once again by a bard, or wandering storyteller, called Ugrashrava Sauti, to a group of sages just before *they* started a long sacrifice, this time for a worthier, more politically correct cause – world peace. It is this new, improved, four-times-the-size-of-the-original version of *Jaya* that we know today as the Mahabharata.

As you have probably noticed, Ugrashrava Sauti's version was *narrated*, not written down. This was generally the way information and stories – even those that were 1.8 million words long – were passed on in the olden days (ancient Indians had insane memory power). The first *written* version – with who knows how many more additions and deletions – that we know, dates back only to the fourth century CE, more than 1,600 years ago.

What makes the Mahabharata more interesting is the belief that it isn't a story that Vyasa made up entirely in his head. It is said to be a mix of fact and fiction, a story set against actual historical events that occurred somewhere around the eighth century BCE (or a lot earlier, or a little later – no one is quite sure. The dating of ancient Indian texts is also often a mix of fact and fiction).

That's really quite enough about the Mahabharata. On to the Gita. Was the conversation between Krishna and Arjuna strictly private, or did anyone else get to eavesdrop on it?

Actually, two people other than the two having the conversation got to hear it too. The interesting part was that these two weren't even on the battlefield at Kurukshetra; they were actually far away, in the Throne Room of the palace of Hastinapura, to be precise. (And how far away was that, exactly? Some 170 km, or about six hours by chariot).

How did people so far away hear a conversation that even people on the battlefield around them didn't hear? Here's how.

On the eve of the Kurukshetra war, King Dhritarashtra was not a happy man. He was bowed down by sorrow at the destruction he knew the war would wreak. He was full of fear that his sons would never return home. He was consumed by guilt that his love for his children had made him so weak that he had neglected his kingly duties and allowed all kinds of terrible injustices to happen right under his nose. Sick at heart, he refused to travel to the battlefield to witness the war.

However, not knowing what was happening there was too much to bear. Enter Sanjaya, the king's charioteer, who had been blessed by Sage Vyasa (yes, the same Vyasa who wrote the Mahabharata) with the gift of telescopic vision and long-distance hearing, besides the gift of being able to see both the past and the future. Sitting beside the nervous king in Hastinapura, Sanjaya saw and heard everything that was happening on the faraway battlefield as clearly as if it were happening before his very eyes. He began to describe, in real time, every teensy-weensy detail of the battle to King Dhritarashtra.

And that was how Sanjaya got to listen in on the Conversation, second-hand, and King Dhritarashtra got to hear it too, third-hand.

And now for one Very Last Formality – the Gita prayer.

Traditionally, before you actually start reading the Gita, you are supposed to send a bunch of prayers up – to the Mahabharata, to its author Vyasa, to the Gita itself and to Krishna – asking for their blessings to help you understand and appreciate its wisdom.

It is a nine-verse prayer, but it is the fourth verse – which explains the importance of the Gita – that is the most quoted. It just wouldn't do to jump to Chapter 1 without at least a basic understanding of this shloka, so let's get it.

सर्वोपनिषदो गावो दोग्धा गोपालनन्दनः।
पार्थो वत्सः सुधीर्भोक्ता दुग्धं गीतामृतं महत्॥

Sarvopanishado gaavo dogdhaa gopaalanandanaha
Paartho vatsas sudhirbhoktaa dugdham
gitaamritam mahat

If all the Upanishads* were cows, Krishna is the divine milkman who squeezes their goodness out. Arjuna, who gets first shot at the distilled wisdom of the ages, is the

---

*A collection of some of India's oldest religious texts, which are believed to be revelations.

calf. The wise and the pure then get to drink this milk, this blessed, immortal nectar that is the Gita.

Got it? Hold that thought. Now, enter the arena and perch on your ringside seat, amid the noise and the heat and the dust. Smell the raw fear and the great courage hanging thick and heavy in the air. Feel the nervous excitement of the soldiers. Hear the whinnying of the horses, the trumpeting of the elephants and the clank of battle armour. See the...

But wait! Something strange is happening. The chariot carrying the great hero breaks away from the ranks and races like the wind to the middle of the field. Our hero slumps to his knees in despair, his mighty bow Gandiva lying uselessly by his side. Krishna looks at his friend with great concern, and begins to speak.

Oops. Hang on a sec. Hit Pause. Rewind a little, to the point before the hero's chariot began to move. Now tune everything else out and, like Sanjaya, focus your senses on nothing else but our hero and his charioteer.

The Conversation is about to begin.

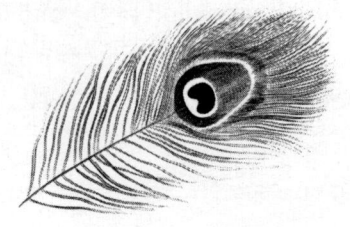

१

the desolation of arjuna ----◀◀◀◆▶▶▶---- arjuna vishada yoga

IN WHICH THE STAGE IS SET FOR THE CONVERSATION

That long-ago day, a nippy dawn was breaking across the sacred field they called Kurukshetra. It was getting to the end of November, and the winter that was already in the air promised to be a harsh one. But the sky, so recently a dull, drab grey, was trying valiantly to infuse some cheer into the morning – awash in peachy pink, edged with gold along the eastern horizon, blending in the west into the fading night in a shade of aubergine. It was a ridiculously pretty sight, designed to melt the most hardened heart, if only its possessor had taken the trouble to cast a glance heavenwards.

As it turned out, no one – yes, not one of the thousands of men gathering on the field – young and old, brave ones and lily-livered ones, the leaders and the followers – bothered with the sky that morning. They were too busy, as men will be, doing Important Things, things that were A Matter of Life and Death, things that were born of hate and greed and fear, and things guaranteed to cause pain and grief and destruction.

They were going to fight a war.

On one side of the field stood the eleven Akshauhinis – giant battalions comprising chariots, elephants, horsemen, and foot soldiers – of the Kaurava army, in precise, gleaming battle formation. Right in the middle, in his golden chariot, stood the supreme commander of the Kaurava forces, Bhishma the Invincible, the oldest man on the field, and the revered and beloved grand uncle of both the Pandavas and the Kauravas.

On the other side of the field were the seven Akshauhinis of the Pandava army – yes, just seven, versus the eleven on the other side. Their smaller number should have left the warriors on this side shaking in their shoes; incredibly, they did not seem to be intimidated in the least, their faces uniformly shining with confidence and hope and good cheer. Not one of them would have bet a single deerskin that he himself would survive the war, but each was quite sure his side would have the eventual victory, for were they not fighting on the side of the good, just and virtuous Pandavas?

If the other side had Bhishma the Invincible, who had the enviable power to choose the time of his own death, did their side not have the supreme battle strategist Krishna? And what about their own commander of the forces, Prince Dhrishtadyumna, brother of Queen Draupadi? The one who, according to the prophecy, was destined to bring down the almighty warrior Drona, guru to both the Pandavas and the Kauravas?

In fact, it was the warriors on the other side who were beginning to look a little jittery as they rubbed their hands and stamped their feet to get the chill out and the blood raging in their veins. They knew that many of the armies that were fighting on their side had been forced to do so – they either owed King Dhritarashtra something, or were bound to fight on the side of Hastinapura for other reasons – and not because they believed that the Kauravas were in the right. Most of them, in fact, believed that the Kauravas had done terrible wrongs – they could not, *would* not, win, especially on a battlefield as sacred as Kurukshetra, known to always favour the good. Such soldiers were not the best people to have on your side in a war, for you never knew when they would lose their spirit.

They also knew that even the great warriors on their side, elders like Bhishma and Drona, who would never do anything cowardly or disloyal, were on the side of the Pandavas in spirit. Bhishma, for instance, had agreed to be commander only on the condition that he would not be expected to kill any of the Pandava brothers. And everyone knew that Guru Drona's most favourite student was none other than the hero of the other side, Arjuna, so it was silly to expect that the revered martial arts teacher to the Kurus and the Pandavas, and one of the few people who *could* bring down Arjuna, would ever actually do so. Oh yes, all things considered, things were looking pretty bleak for the Kauravas, despite their eleven Akshauhinis.

This sense of impending doom was not limited to the battlefield either. Far away in the Throne Room of Hastinapura, King Dhritarashtra was feeling it too. His head told him that his 100 mighty sons, backed by great war heroes, powerful regional kings and Krishna's own powerful Yadava army – the Narayani Sena – could not but win. But his heart knew that the Pandavas, all legendary warriors themselves, had not only truth and justice but Krishna himself on their side – and it whispered that the Kauravas could not but lose.

The Lord of the Bharata clan turned to his charioteer, the clairvoyant Sanjaya, who had been blessed with divine vision and hearing to enable him to see and hear the events unfolding on the battlefield, and began to speak. 'Tell me, Sanjaya,' he said, 'what is going on in that holy field of Kurukshetra, where my sons and the sons of my brother Pandu have gathered to fight?'

Sanjaya focused his senses on the battlefield. He saw Duryodhana's brow furrow in worry as he took in, for the first time, the splendour and size of the Pandava army. He saw the Kaurava's jaw clench as he made a decision, and saw him walk purposefully towards his guru Drona. And Sanjaya began to describe the scene, as it unfolded, to his impatient master.

Duryodhana was not often nervous, but today was different. Those blasted cousins of his had managed to put together quite a mighty army, after all. He would have to talk to his commanders, some of whom he knew despised him and loved the Pandavas. He would have to provoke them, remind them of things that they would rather forget, make them abandon their good judgement and plunge into the war with blind fury, determined to bring down the opposition, no matter who they were. Also, although he would never admit it even to himself, Duryodhana wanted to be reassured that his side still had as good a chance of winning as he had earlier believed.

He headed straightaway towards his guru, Dronacharya. 'Guruji,' he said, 'do you see the great army on the other side, put together by your students, the Pandava brothers? Do you see how expertly their battalions have been arranged by another of your students, the sharp, intelligent Dhrishtadyumna?'

Out of the corner of his eye, Duryodhana saw his guru's hand tighten on his bow. There! His words had had the desired effect. What kind of disciples – indeed, what kind of men – were the Pandavas if they were willing to raise arms against their own teacher?

Duryodhana chuckled inwardly. The mention of Dhrishtadyumna was a master stroke too. Dhrishtadyumna was the son of Drona's sworn enemy, and it had been prophesied that he would kill Drona some day. Nothing like a reminder of your own death to get the old adrenaline pumping.

'Do you see,' Duryodhana went on, 'the many heroic warriors on that side, even apart from Bhima and Arjuna? There's Dhrishtaketu, Shaibya, Kuntibhoja, Yudhamanyu, Uttamauja, Abhimanyu . . .'

He trailed off, allowing the scale of the challenge that faced them to sink in. Then he quickly changed tack. It would not do for his commanders to become demoralized, after all.

'Of course,' he went on smoothly, 'it isn't as if our side doesn't have great leaders. There's you, Karna, Kripa, Vikarna and your own son, Ashwatthama. There are several other heroes, all loyal to me, fully prepared to give up their lives. And best of all, we are protected by the Pitamaha, Grandfather Bhishma. If all our commanders make sure that he is kept safe, we should be all right.'

Duryodhana paused, waiting for the Acharya's reaction. He had spoken confidently, but he wasn't sure that his side was going to be fine at all. 'We *should* be fine, right, Acharya? Right?' he transmitted wordlessly. If Drona caught the mute plea in his student's eyes, he did not show it. Nor did he respond.

But someone else did, someone whose old eyes had seen generations of men come and go, and whose large, compassionate heart held in it equal parts of love for all his grandsons. Standing tall on his chariot, the supreme commander of the Kurus filled his lungs, roared like a lion, and blew loud and long into his conch, silencing the doubters, shattering every last hope of peace and

conciliation, proclaiming to earth and heaven that the Kauravas were ready to fight to the death.

Joy, excitement and renewed hope raced through Duryodhana and down the ranks of the Kaurava army like a cold fire. A great clamour broke out, and the sound of bugles, trumpets and drums rent the air. Victory would be theirs! Of *course* it would!

But wait, what was that? From the far side of the field, from another golden chariot drawn by four white horses and proudly flying the flag of Hanuman, came the sound of not one, but two conches, blown lustily and in unison. Every man on the field froze – these were no ordinary conches; the conch-blowers were no ordinary men either.

The early morning mist had evaporated, but a sudden unearthly chill rose out of nowhere to envelop the Kaurava army.

'O King,' said Sanjaya, 'there is Krishna, blowing his divine Panchajanya, and there, beside him, is Arjuna, blowing his Devadutta. Down the field, Bhima of the insatiable appetite puts down his mace and joins in on his Paundra, just as Yudhishthira lays aside his lance to sound his victory conch, the Anantavijaya. The twins, Nakula the Handsome and Sahadeva, Master of the Swords, not to be outdone, are blowing their own conches, the melodious Sughosha and the jewelled Manipushpaka. Now Virata, Shikhandi, Dhrishtadyumna, Satyaki, the sons of Draupadi, and the strong-armed son of Subhadra – Abhimanyu – have joined in too.'

In spite of himself, Dhritarashtra shuddered. Sanjaya noticed it, but being clairvoyant, able to see what had been and what would be, he had no words of comfort to offer his master. He felt a great pity for the blind king, but knew in his heart that the Lord of the

Kurus had only himself to blame for letting things come to this. Should he keep some of the less savoury details of the battle about to begin from the king, then? But that decision was not Sanjaya's to make — he was only the commentator, the impartial observer, and it was his duty to report without emotion on everything that was going on. But oh, it was hard not to be able to express an opinion or take sides, not to wail and lament the coming destruction of a great kingdom.

He let his gaze travel over the faces of the 100 Kaurava princes. Sighing inwardly, he steeled himself to convey what he saw to the king.

'The uproar is tumultuous,' he said. 'It rents the earth and the sky, and it shatters the hearts of the sons of Dhritarashtra.'

IN WHICH THE WARRIOR LEAVES THE FIELD (AT LEAST IN SPIRIT)

Arjuna put down his conch and picked up his trusty bow, the Gandiva. The uproar on the battlefield had excited his warrior blood and he was raring to go. A sudden urge to suss out the opposition one last time, to see what he was really up against, came over him. It would not hurt for the opposition to see him in his full glory either – broad-shouldered, slim-hipped, golden in the sunrise, Arjuna the Atimaharathi, who could hold off an entire Akshauhini on his own, their own personal angel of doom coming to get them. He cracked a smile at the thought.

'Krishna,' he said, tapping his charioteer on the shoulder, 'do me a favour, will you? We still have a few minutes before everyone starts shooting. Drive me right into the centre of the battlefield, bang into the middle of both armies. Who *are* these people who want to help my rotten cousin Duryodhana achieve his evil ends? I want to lock eyes with them, stare them down, scare them silly, before I grind them into the dust.'

Krishna chuckled. 'Show-off!'

Arjuna shrugged. 'Can't really help it if I am the greatest archer in the world, can I?'

Krishna's eyebrows disappeared into his crown.

'What?' bristled Arjuna, suddenly insecure. 'I am, aren't I? I mean, I know Karna is good too, but everyone knows I'm the best, and Acharya himself has said that, in so many words. You don't agree?'

'Calm down, Atimaharathi!' smiled Krishna, 'Just teasing you. I can't believe you fall for it every time!' Dodging Arjuna's playful punch, he tugged at the reins and clicked his tongue. The horses took off, their white manes flying as they galloped to the centre of the field. Krishna steered the chariot into position and turned to look at his friend.

'All yours. Stare away!'

Smiling smugly, Arjuna surveyed the opposition. Before him, stretching away into the distance on either side, arrayed in glittering, seemingly endless rows, were the eleven Akshauhinis of the Kaurava army, impatient for the war to begin. Squinting to be able to see more clearly, he zoomed in on the faces of the commanders in their gilded chariots, the teams of expert bowmen in the gaily painted howdahs, the leaders of the cavalry, and the frontrunners of the vast infantry.

They were all people he recognized – fathers and grandfathers who had watched over him in his childhood – scolding, pampering, advising, praising – uncles and cousins who had been a vital part of his teenage years, teachers and elders – including Grandfather Bhishma, who had been more than a father to him, and his beloved Acharya Drona, who had taught him all he knew. There were nephews and grandnephews whom he had dandled on his knee, fathers-in-law and brothers-in-law who had made him feel welcome in their own families, distant relatives with whom he remembered spending many pleasant evenings, and scores of close friends that he had competed, argued, studied and laughed with for more years than he could remember.

And he, Arjuna, was here to stare them down, before he let fly his unerring arrows and cut them down.

Suddenly, the enormity of what he was about to do struck Arjuna like a thunderbolt. The greatest archer in the world broke into a cold sweat. A deadly fear he had never before encountered paralysed his mind. His knees buckled under him and his hands shook uncontrollably, letting the Gandiva slip from his grasp.

'Krishna,' he whispered in a voice he barely recognized as his own. 'I cannot do this.'

Krishna whirled in his seat, took one look at Arjuna's ashen face and realized something was very wrong. 'What is it, Arjuna? What can you not do?'

'This,' Arjuna swept his arm in a wide arc, taking in the entire Kuru army. 'The war, the bloodshed, the killing, everything.'

Krishna waited.

'This is not the enemy, Krishna. Enemies do not have the faces of my friends or my closest family.' Arjuna shook his head in disbelief. 'What was I *thinking*? Did I really imagine that I could destroy my nearest and dearest with my own hands? That I would cover myself in glory by killing my brothers and fathers? That a kingdom – a piece of unfeeling earth – would be worth the ravaging of everything and everyone I hold dear?'

Arjuna paused, unable to go on, his face a mask of self-loathing. 'What would be the point of untold riches, Krishna, if they were tainted with the blood of my family, if the people I want to share them with were no longer around? What god am I trying to please with this bloody sacrifice? What sin can be greater than fratricide, unless it is the sin of murdering your teacher? And here I am, all set to do both, *eager* to do both. Yeah, rather heroic, that!'

A dark cloud of depression settled heavily on the warrior's shoulders, weighing him down. Krishna's heart went out to him, and he opened his mouth to speak, but Arjuna cut him short. 'Don't say it. Don't say that the other side is all set to commit fratricide as well, and that's what they *will* do if we don't fight back. That's a stupid argument. We all know, have always known, that Duryodhana is immoral and devious and greedy and unjust, and that his brothers follow him mindlessly. How are we – the so-called "noble" Pandavas – any better than he is if we do exactly what he does, even though we know it is undeniably, unforgivably wrong? Go on then, tell me honestly, what is the difference between us and *them*?

'No, Krishna,' Arjuna went on hopelessly, not pausing to hear his friend's answer. 'Orphaned grandchildren, widowed mothers and daughters, an entire generation of brothers and nephews gone, the kingdom destroyed, a land at the mercy of lawless criminals and rogues, where women are not safe . . .' Arjuna paused, his voice choking on a sob, 'nothing, *nothing*, is worth that.

'I'm sorry, Krishna, but I'd rather die in battle, unresisting and unarmed, than raise my bow against a single one of my kinsmen.'

'Thus spoke Arjuna, O Jewel of the Bharata Clan,' reported Sanjaya, 'before sinking to the seat of his chariot, and casting away his bow and quiver, his heart overcome with sorrow.'

Dhritarashtra started in his seat, staring sightlessly into the distance, a forlorn hope coursing through his veins. Arjuna, the great hero, the single biggest threat to the Kuru army, had laid down arms? Maybe there was still hope for his sons, then! Maybe the Pandavas, who were sometimes too noble, and too foolish, for their own good, would walk away from the war, and the entire kingdom would once again belong to his own sons! Maybe ...

But Sanjaya was speaking again. 'To him who was thus overcome by sorrow, to him whose eyes brimmed over with tears and whose spirit was despondent, Krishna spoke thus ...'

The very first shloka of the Gita

Guess whose voice opens the Gita? Nope, not Krishna's, and not Arjuna's either. In fact, it is the voice of the anxious King Dhritarashtra, who asks Sanjaya a question. Interestingly, this is the only time in the entire Gita that Dhritarashtra speaks.

धृतराष्ट्र उवाच ।
धर्मक्षेत्रे कुरुक्षेत्रे समवेता युयुत्सवः ।
मामकाः पाण्डवाश्चैव किमकुर्वत संजय ॥१-१॥

Dhritarashtra uvaacha
Dharmakshetrey kurukshetrey samavetaa yuyutsavaha
maamakaah paandavaashchaiva kimakurvata Sanjaya

Thus spoke Dhritarashtra: 'O Sanjaya, tell me what is going on in that holy field of Kurukshetra, where my sons and the Pandavas have gathered to fight?' (1-1)

Armies in ancient India

In the olden days, the armies of the land essentially comprised four divisions – chariots, elephants, cavalry (soldiers on horseback) and infantry (foot soldiers). All four divisions were represented even in the smallest, most basic unit of a battalion – the Patti. Pattis built up to form Sena-Mukhas, Sena-Mukhas were grouped together to form Gulmas, and so on, all the way up to a massive battle formation called an Akshauhini. Here's how it worked.

1 PATTI

5   1   3   1

1 chariot (Ratha) + 1 elephant (Gaja) + 3 horses (Ashva) + 5 foot soldiers (Padhata) = 1 Patti

3 Pattis = 1 Sena-Mukha

3 Sena-Mukhas = 1 Gulma

3 Gulmas = 1 Gana

3 Ganas = 1 Vahini

3 Vahinis = 1 Pruthana

3 Pruthanas = 1 Chamu

3 Chamus = 1 Anikini

10 Anikini = 1 Big Fat Akshauhini!

So how many chariots/elephants in an Akshauhini? How many horses? And foot soldiers? Try and work it out for yourself before you read on for the answers.

And the right answer is ... There are 21,870 chariots, 21,870 elephants, 65,610 cavalry and 109,350 infantry in 1 Akshauhini.

So if the Kauravas had 11 Akshauhinis, they had 240,570 chariots, 240,570 elephants, 721,710 horses and 1,202,850 infantry, versus the Pandavas' seven Akshauhinis with 153,090 chariots, 153,090 elephants, 459,270 horses, and 765,450 infantry. Even assuming just one person per chariot and one person per elephant – typically, there were at least two in a chariot and at least six on an elephant – there were close to a whopping four million men fighting in the Great War!

On another note, did you notice something about the Akshauhini numbers? Whether you take the number of chariots (21870), or the elephants (21870), or the cavalry (65610) or the foot soldiers (109350), the digits always add up to 18! And there are 18 Parvas (books) in the Mahabharata, and 18 chapters in the Gita, and, best of all, the Kurukshetra War lasted exactly 18 days. Cool, huh?

Look out! It's an Atimaharathi!

Warriors in ancient India, or at least in the Mahabharata, were graded according to their skill. The greatest warriors rode in chariots, to which they graduated from horseback. With their own personal chauffeurs – the Sarathis* – these warriors were then free to concentrate on doing what they did best – bringing down the enemy with all the weapons at their command.

*For a warrior, the Sarathi of his chariot often made the difference between life and death. Steering the chariot – and the warrior – away from a flaming arrow or similar missile, urging the horses speedily through the opposition ranks, and being an extra pair of eyes for the warrior, a good Sarathi was an invaluable asset in battle. Having bagged Krishna for his Sarathi, Arjuna was in very good hands indeed.

But even among chariot riders, or Rathis, there were levels of excellence. An **Atirathi** was the lowliest, a warrior capable of fighting off a mere 10,000 warriors (whether on foot or on horseback) at a time. Next in the pecking order were the **Maharathis**, heroes like Duryodhana, Dhrishtadyumna, Ashwatthama, Abhimanyu, and all the Pandava brothers except Arjuna, who were capable of holding up to 60,000 warriors simultaneously. Superior to them were the **Atimaharathis** – men like Arjuna, Karna, Bhishma and Drona – who no longer dealt with lowly foot soldiers but focused purely on Maharathis, being able to single-handedly take on a dozen of them at a time!

There was also another, even more superior class of Rathis, called the **Mahamaharathis**, who were capable of fighting 24 Atimaharathi warriors at the same time! But no mortal ever attained this status, mainly because there never were 24 Atimaharathis at the same place at the same time, ever. In theory, though, gods and their avatars – Shiva, Rama, Krishna – are believed to be Mahamaharathis.

Yes, sir. No, sir. We're here to fight a war, sir.

Wars in ancient India were fought according to a strict code of ethical and humane laws that were fair both to the combatants and to those who stayed at home. Here is a quick rundown of some of those rules, several of which were broken during the course of the Kurukshetra war.

- Fighting must begin no earlier than sunrise and should end exactly at sunset.
- More than one warrior must not attack a single warrior.
- Two warriors may duel, or engage in prolonged personal combat, only if they carry the same weapons and are on the same mount (a chariot warrior cannot attack a horseman, for instance)
- No warrior may kill or injure a warrior who has surrendered.
- A warrior who surrenders becomes a prisoner of war and will then be entitled to the privileges of a prisoner of war.
- No warrior may kill or injure an unarmed warrior.
- No warrior may kill or injure an unconscious warrior.
- No warrior may kill or injure a person or animal not taking part in the war.
- No warrior may kill or injure a warrior whose back is towards him.

- No warrior may strike an animal not considered a direct threat.
- The rules specific to each weapon must be followed. For example, it is prohibited to strike below the waist in mace warfare.
- Warriors must not engage in any 'unfair' warfare whatsoever.
- The lives of women, prisoners of war and farmers are sacred.
- Land should not be pillaged.

Almost too good to be true, what? War is no fun for anyone, in any age, but how much more civilized does this kind of war sound compared to today's night-time drone attacks on civilian targets?

War games

Does the Akshauhini battalion, with its chariots, elephants, horses and men, remind you of something? Yup, it is what the ancient Indian game of Chaturanga – the original version of chess – is based on. Continuing with that thought, would you say five-time World Chess Champion Viswanathan Anand is an Atimaharathi?

२

the yoga of knowledge ----◄◄◄◆►►►---- sankhya yoga

IN WHICH KRISHNA GIVES ARJUNA A STERN TALKING-TO

'Shame on you, Arjuna!'

The words were uttered quietly, but there was no mistaking the rebuke in Krishna's tone.

'Greatest archer in the world, he calls himself! Noblest of warriors, destroyer of foes, most single-minded of men! Ha!'

The hunched figure on the floor of the chariot refused to be provoked. Instead, Arjuna seemed to sink further into himself.

'Oh, come on! You knew all along what this war was about, whom you were going to fight. You've had enough time to debate the rightness and wrongness of it before the decision to fight was made. You cannot start thinking about it *now*, when you are already on the battlefield, when your side is depending on you to lead them to victory!'

Krishna waited, hoping for some kind of reaction. None came.

'This is completely disgraceful behaviour for a warrior, and you know it. There is no honour in running away from battle, and dejection does not suit you.' Krishna's voice grew sterner. 'Enough of that snivelling, Arjuna. Stand up, pick up your bow and fight a battle worthy of a Pandava prince!'

'Do stop, Krishna!' begged Arjuna. 'Do you even realize what you're asking of me? Slaughtering my brothers, murdering my teachers – how can that be noble or right, in *any* universe?' Arjuna shook his head incredulously. 'Why, every holy scripture I have ever read roundly condemns such killing as the most terrible of sins. Every moment of my life beyond such a war will be stained with blood-guilt and utter despair. Don't you see how . . .?'

Arjuna stopped. His arguments had begun to sound weak and hollow, even to his own ears. For Arjuna came from a proud bloodline of fighting men, and both his natural warrior instincts and years of rigorous training had been waiting a lifetime to find expression in a war exactly like this one. Every fibre of his being reaffirmed to him that it would only be the worst kind of coward who ran away from the battlefield, even though fleeing seemed a very tempting proposition, even a *noble* one, at the moment. If he followed his impulse and ran, though, would he be able to live with himself?

But the alternative – not running away, staying and fighting and killing the people most dear to him –

was equally terrible to contemplate. Lost in a fog of utter bewilderment, Arjuna did what he had always done over the years in such situations. He turned to his closest friend and his wisest mentor, the only one in the world he completely trusted, and placed the dilemma in his hands.

'I have no answers, Krishna. I cannot see my way forward. You have never let me down before and I know you will not now. Help me, my friend. Tell me, straight up and without mincing your words, what I should do.'

There was a pause. Krishna waited, sensing he wasn't quite done yet.

A moment later, Arjuna lifted his chin defiantly, a touch of the old haughtiness back in the handsome face. 'Let me clarify one thing, Krishna, before you speak. You know I trust your judgment, but I will need to be fully convinced by your point of view. Otherwise,' he locked eyes with Krishna, 'I will not fight.'

Krishna smiled. 'Listen then, my dearest Arjuna . . .'

Lessons from the Gita

1. It's not only okay to be confused, it's a darned good thing.

2. Now that you are confused, don't look outside for help, look inside.

Krishna's smile is an important turning point in the Conversation. Krishna is amused at Arjuna's attempts to find excuses for his sudden weakness on the battlefield, but pleased that he has finally stopped arguing and accepted that he does not know what to do. There is no shame in admitting that you don't know what's right; in fact, it is the first step to figuring out what is.

So how do you figure what's right? Do you ask people around you, and listen to anyone who has an opinion and is willing to share it? Absolutely not, says the Gita. Instead, it exhorts you to be like Arjuna.

Arjuna knows that if he walks away from the battlefield, his opponents will snigger at him, calling him a coward who got cold feet at the sight of their mighty army. His brothers, wives and children, not to mention his teachers and elders, will be disappointed in him. The army he is supposed to lead will be embarrassed by his desertion and furious at his betrayal, and history will label him a traitor. If he stays and fights, however, everyone will call him a hero and sing his praises, and generations of men to follow will revere him as a great warrior. Given these two options, most people would have picked the second one without a moment's thought.

The fact that Arjuna *didn't*, is what makes him worthy. It wasn't what *other* people thought that mattered to him, it was what he himself felt, in his own heart. But his heart was completely at war with itself! That's when Arjuna made his second good decision. He didn't simply close out one bad option and choose the other, saying, 'I'll think about the wisdom of it all later, once the war is done.' Instead, he decided to resolve his inner conflict right then and there, never mind how long it took or how inconvenient it would make things for him and, possibly, everyone else. He simply put his bow down and turned to Krishna for advice.

And so can you.

How?

Who is Krishna, anyway? And where can you find him?

In the Gita, which is the holy book of the Hindus, Krishna is portrayed as God Himself, and God is portrayed as man's best and closest friend, someone he can talk to about anything, and whose advice, given with love and understanding, he can trust completely. In fact, whenever Sanjaya reports on what Krishna is saying, he refers to him not by name but as *Sri Bhagavan*, the Blessed Lord.

If you find the idea of talking to God strange, you can talk instead to your conscience, your own inner voice, which usually knows what the right thing to do in a given situation is. All you need to do is to shut out the deafening voice that fills your head, saying, 'But will others think I'm weird / a scaredy cat / not cool enough / not fun enough / stupid / a goody two-shoes?', and you will hear your quiet inner voice, giving you the right advice.

Try it the next time you are confused about what to do in a tough situation. It may not always be easy to follow that advice – more often than not, it will be very difficult. Obeying your inner voice may not always make you happy or popular or cool at the time, but later, you will be content, knowing that it was the right thing to have done. And that's what really counts.

Echoes of the Gita

In the American coming-of-age novel, To Kill A Mockingbird by Harper Lee, seven-year-old Scout's lawyer father Atticus takes a decision to defend a black man against a white man in court. The story is set in the 1930s, in a small, conservative town in Alabama, a part of the USA that was highly racist at the time. The white population of the town is furious with Atticus, and Scout and her older brother Jem bear the brunt of their insults. One day, Scout asks her father exactly why he was taking on such a controversial case:

> 'Well, most folks seem to think that they're right and you're wrong...'
>
> 'They're certainly entitled to think that, and they're entitled to full respect for their opinions,' said Atticus, 'but before I can live with other folks, I've got to live with myself. The one thing that doesn't abide by majority rule is a person's conscience.'

Atticus goes on to fight the case, and lose. But his children never forget the lesson in courage and conviction that he taught them by his actions.

And Krishna said, 'Why do you grieve, Arjuna? Don't; there is no need for sorrow. You can't really kill anyone, you know – neither your venerable grandfather nor your beloved Acharya, neither your cousins nor your friends. Even you, Atimaharathi, do not have that power.'

Arjuna's head shot up in surprise. 'What do you mean? When I shoot my arrows into them, will they not hurt nor bleed? Will they not fall to the ground, these men, never to rise again? I don't know what you call it, Krishna, but I call it murder, plain and simple.'

'Ah, that's because you aren't seeing the true picture, Arjuna,' Krishna said. 'What is birth, really? What is death? Do you imagine that before we were born, we didn't exist? Of course we did, in some other form. After we die, do we cease to exist? Not really. We continue to exist, but in yet another form, that's all. Does that make sense?'

Arjuna shook his head.

'Look at it from a different angle. What is it that really dies when a person dies? Only his physical body. But his soul, his Atman, which is the true essence of him, the untouchable, invisible spirit of him – now *that* . . . cannot be destroyed, ever. If you imagine that you can "kill" someone's Atman, there is no greater fool than you.'

The Great Archer's brow furrowed. He wanted so badly to believe what his friend was saying, but Krishna's argument was simply not working for him.

'Think of it this way, Arjuna,' Krishna tried again. 'The body is just a temporary home for the soul. Just as we change our clothes, the soul changes bodies, casting off its old one to take on a new one. The soul itself is indestructible, unchangeable.

'Now that you know you can do no real harm to your nearest and dearest, why are you worried? Just go out there and fight!'

But Arjuna was far from convinced. 'Atman, indestructible, unchangeable – comforting words, Krishna, and they may even be true if you are saying them. But what solace is it to me to know that at the end of the war, I will only have destroyed my brothers' bodies and not their immortal souls? I would still have lost them as I know them, wouldn't I?'

Krishna shrugged. 'Okay, let's have it your way then. Let's say that you *have* lost them forever. But didn't you always know you would lose them some day? Of course you did! Did you actually believe that you could hold on to them for all eternity? Of course you didn't. Listen, Arjuna, death is certain for anything that is born, and new birth is certain for anything that is dead. Now, tell me, does a wise man lament over something so inevitable?'

Lessons from the Gita

3. Matter cannot be created or destroyed; it only changes form.

If you are in the eighth grade or older, you probably recognize this as something you studied in Physics – yup, it's called 'The Law of Conservation of Matter'. The American astronomer Carl Sagan put it in a more goosebumpy way in his book *Cosmos*, where he says: 'The nitrogen in our DNA, the calcium in our teeth, the iron in our blood, and the carbon in our apple pies were made in the interiors of collapsing stars. We are made of starstuff.'

And to starstuff we shall return. Just like everything else in the Universe. Yes, including the dinosaurs.

So what happened to that starstuff that was in the dinosaurs? It got broken down and scattered about when they died, then regrouped in different ways to form us, millions of years later.

In the Gita, Krishna says essentially the same thing in these two verses.

न त्वेवाहं जातु नासं न त्वं नेमे जनाधिपाः ।
न चैव न भविष्यामः सर्वे वयमतः परम् ॥२-१२॥

Na tvevaaham jaatu naasam na tvam neymey
janaadhipaahaa
Na chaiva na bhavishyaamah sarvey vayamatah
param

Never was there a time when I did not exist, nor you, nor all these kings before you; and neither will any of us cease to be in the future. (2-12)

नासतो विद्यते भावो नाभावो विद्यते सतः ।
उभयोरपि दृष्टोऽन्तस्त्वनयोस्तत्त्वदर्शिभिः ॥२-१६॥

Naasato vidyatey bhaavo naabhaavo vidyatey sataha ubhayorapi drishton-tas-tv-anayos-tattva-darshibhihi

All the wise seers have discovered this truth: of the non-existent there is no coming to be; of the existent there is no ceasing to be. (2-16)

So exactly what we are saying here – that what the Hindus call reincarnation – the process by which, they believe, the soul of a dead person is reborn in another person's body – is what scientists call The Law of Conservation of Matter? Umm, that would be oversimplifying it, but yes, they are both essentially the same *idea*. There is *something* – call it energy, life force, Atman – that is within us, that can never be destroyed.

Science generally looks down its nose at Spirituality, casting it aside as a load of fanciful nonsense, and

Spirituality is constantly annoyed with Science for demanding 'proof' before it can believe in anything, but if they both sat down across a table and talked, they may find they have more in common than they realize!

It wasn't working. Logical arguments about death and dying were all very well when you were sitting in a comfortable room and talking about a hypothetical situation, but they fell flat when you were about to begin a battle, where real people would die by your hand.

Krishna decided to change tack. If Arjuna wanted emotion instead of logic, he would get it.

'Think about who you are, Son of Kunti,' he said. 'You are a Kshatriya, member of a proud caste whose most basic duty is to engage in battle to defend what is good and just. Your very Dharma, your bounden duty, is to maintain order, by force if necessary. Running away to the mountains to meditate is simply not an option for your tribe.

'In fact,' Krishna went on, 'you should be delighted at the opportunity that has presented itself before you. Not every Kshatriya gets to fight a lawful battle – you know very clearly which side is in the wrong here. It doesn't happen very often – usually, right and wrong are a fuzzy business. Here's your open door to heaven, Arjuna – fight to your potential, do your duty and win a place there. Turn your back on the fight, and you will be committing a sin.'

Fear jumped into Arjuna's eyes. Krishna saw it, and dug in mercilessly.

'Oh, and I'm not even going to start on the dishonour you will bring upon yourself if you do not fight. The bigger they are, the harder they fall, Partha, and you are the biggest there is. For a man like you, disrepute is a hundred times worse than death, and you, my friend, will not survive the shame, trust me. Die in battle and you rise to heaven; win and you conquer the earth. It's a no-brainer. Come on, get up and fight!'

Krishna did not really believe that Arjuna would leap up and plunge into battle at his words, and Arjuna didn't. Shrewdly, Krishna changed tack once again.

'There is only one trick in the book, Arjuna,' he said. 'Learn it, and your every confusion will be instantly resolved. Master it, and you will be free.'

Arjuna raised his head, his eyes full of hope. 'You're not teasing me again, are you, Krishna?'

Krishna shook his head slowly.

'Fine friend *you* are turning out to be!' scolded Arjuna, feigning anger. 'If the answer to my confusion was that simple, why have you been holding out on me all this while? Teach it to me now, quickly! I am weary of this conflict that rages in my head. Go on – what *is* it?'

The Compassionate Lord smiled to himself. Impatient, beloved Arjuna, gifted man of action, brilliant student who had quickly perfected every skill his teachers had sought to teach him, so confident of mastering every trick in the book. Ah, Partha, he chuckled to himself, I suspect this particular trick will require rather more work than the others.

'Listen then, Arjuna,' began Krishna, looking fondly into his friend's eager, upturned face.

IN WHICH KRISHNA SHARES WITH ARJUNA A KILLER APP FOR CONTENTMENT

'The trick,' said Krishna, 'is to do your duty with single-minded focus and great sincerity, *without worrying about the results of the work.*'

Arjuna frowned. What Krishna was saying seemed straightforward enough, in theory, but how easy was it in practice?

'The trick is not to think about whether your work will be a success or a failure, whether it will please anyone or not, even whether it will make you happy or not, because thinking of results when you should be working will only distract you from the work itself.

'Men who do this, who think only about the higher purpose of the work and not about the results of that work, Arjuna, are Sthitapragyas – men who are happy in the now, always.'

Arjuna shook his head. 'I need more details, Krishna, to picture such a happy man in my head. What does he look like, then, this Sthitapragya? What might he say when I meet him? How will I recognize him?'

'This is a man, Partha, who is free of desire. He doesn't need anything from the world to be happy; he is happy in himself. Even in the midst of sorrow, his mind is calm and untroubled. He is hardly ever highly excited about anything, and seldom fearful or angry. You will not see him rejoicing after a triumph, or grieving for a defeat. He treats everyone – people who like him, people who don't, people who serve him, people whom he serves – with the same affection and respect.'

'I like him already!' said Arjuna. 'But how did he get there, this man, to his Sthitapragya state?'

'It's really all about controlling the senses, Partha. You see, most men seek to feed their senses endlessly – they want to be surrounded by beautiful things (sight), harmonious sounds (hearing), delicious food (taste), agreeable scents (smell) and luxurious textures (touch). They think about these "sense objects" all the time.

'If you think about such objects endlessly, you begin to get fond of them (attachment). Once you get fond of something, you want it for yourself (desire). If you can't have it for some reason, or if someone else has it, you get upset (anger). When you are upset and angry, your brain gets fuddled (confusion). You can't think straight any more, you lose the ability to make rational judgements, and you end up doing something that's silly, hurtful, or plain unethical (destruction of intelligence).'

Arjuna nodded. He knew all this from personal experience, of course, but he liked the logical way Krishna broke it down.

'The Sthitapragya understands this sequence of events well, understands that it all begins with the senses,' said Krishna. 'Just as a tortoise withdraws its limbs into its shell and goes still, he withdraws his senses into himself, and is therefore calm.

'Just like the mighty ocean is completely undisturbed even as the waters of countless rivers empty into it, so is a Sthitapragya – his mind completely unruffled even as desires flow into it from every side.'

Lessons from the Gita

4. Eureka! There IS a recipe for happiness!

Like all of us, Arjuna was human, and as humans, we are all enmeshed in a world full of opposites – pleasure and pain, joy and sorrow, profit and loss, victory and defeat, success and failure, birth and death. We work and sweat and plot and plan and spend all our time trying to achieve one side of each pair of opposites – pleasure, joy, profit, victory, success – while avoiding the other – pain, sorrow, loss, defeat, failure.

But here's the thing – both sides are really not all that different from each other. What's more, *one cannot exist without the other*. It's only because we think of something as pleasurable that its absence becomes what we think of as painful. It's only because we believe the world when it tells us we have lost that we believe it once again when it tells us we have won.

Do you see how it works? You *cannot* avoid the 'bad' side of the equation, because rejecting the 'bad' side means denying the 'good' side as well. Have you noticed that when you get something without working too hard for it (without suffering 'pain'), you don't feel half as much pleasure as you would if you had? On the flip side, if you haven't wanted or loved or enjoyed something very much, you don't miss it when it's gone. More importantly, neither side ever lasts – not pleasure, not pain, not victory, not defeat.

So what should you do? Accept both sides of each pair of opposites with the same sunny attitude? Yes. But here's another way of achieving the same result – *reject* both sides of each pair of opposites! Whichever one you pick, it means the same thing – you neither get elated when something 'good' happens, nor depressed when something 'bad' happens. You're always calm. And being calm means no fear (of failure), no desire (for victory), no sorrow (over loss), and no anger (at rejection).

Isn't it very hard to accept or reject every pair of opposites, especially since our entire world is made up of them? You bet it is. But one simple way to start on the long, long journey there is to stay completely focused on the work at hand, whatever that work may be – studying for an exam, helping your parents around the house, taking care of a cranky grandparent, researching a science project with teammates you don't get along with... Don't think about how disagreeable the work is, don't wonder what the point of it is, don't worry about whether it will bring you the rewards – or the failures – that you hope, or dread, that it will. Instead, put your head down and 'Just do it'.

Eventually, the work itself will become the purpose, and you will not care about the results. The work itself will become the reward, and you will stop looking outside it for rewards.

On the surface, it may seem like a recipe for a dull life, but those who have tried it swear it is actually a recipe for perfect and lasting happiness.

If

Rudyard Kipling
(Excerpt)

> If you can dream – and not make dreams your master;
> If you can think – and not make thoughts your aim;
> If you can meet with Triumph and Disaster
> And treat those two impostors just the same;
>
> If you can talk with crowds and keep your virtue,
> Or walk with Kings – nor lose the common touch,
> If neither foes nor loving friends can hurt you,
> If all men count with you, but none too much;
>
> If you can fill the unforgiving minute
> With sixty seconds' worth of distance run,

Yours is the Earth and everything that's in it,
And – which is more – you'll be a Man, my son!

If the Gita's philosophy were reduced to one shloka . . .

. . . it would be Shloka 47 of the second chapter of the Gita. Understandably, it is also one of the most famous of the 700 shlokas. Many Hindus, even those who don't know much else about the Gita, will be able to quote at least part of this shloka. Here it is in its original form for you to enjoy.

कर्मण्येवाधिकारस्ते मा फलेषु कदाचन ।
मा कर्मफलहेतुर्भूर्मा ते सङ्गोऽस्त्वकर्मणि ॥२-४७॥

Karmanye-vaadhi-kaarastey maa phaleshu kadaachana
Maa karma-phala-hetur-bhoor-maa tey sango-stva-karmani

You only have the right to perform your duty, but you are not entitled to the fruits of your action. Never consider yourself the cause of the results of your activities and do not be attached to inaction. (2-47)

3

the yoga of work ◀◀◀◆▶▶▶ karma yoga

IN WHICH KRISHNA MORE OR LESS BLOCKS ARJUNA'S ESCAPE ROUTE

'Hold on a minute, Janardhana,' said Arjuna, looking more confused than ever. 'For a while there, I thought I understood what you were saying, but you've lost me again. On the one hand, you are saying I should withdraw my senses and become a Sthitapragya who wants nothing from the world, and on the other, you are urging me to get so trapped by worldly ambition that I should not hesitate to fight a bloody war and kill my closest family for the sake of a kingdom!

'In one breath, you say that I should walk the path of knowledge and look inwards to find my peace, in the next, you ask me to take the path of action, to go out and commit acts of violence. Can you stop saying contradictory things and tell me, once and for all, which is the better path?'

'The truth is, Partha,' Krishna said, 'that there is no "better" path. Both paths – the path of knowledge and the path of action – work just as well. It is up to you to pick the one that you are suited to.

'The path of knowledge works for the thinkers – the quiet, thoughtful ones who delight in the pursuits of the mind; the path of action,' Krishna looked pointedly at his friend, 'works for the doers – the active, energetic extroverts who find their greatest pleasure in throwing themselves into something physical.'

'That makes me sound a bit of a brute,' said Arjuna. 'I'm sure I can be quiet and thoughtful too; I'm sure I can give up this terrible "action" you seem to think I'm so suited to and retreat to the forest to meditate and walk the path of knowledge.'

'Ah, Partha, if only it were that easy to "give up" action!' said Krishna. 'Think about it – can anyone attached to a living body honestly claim to have abandoned action altogether? Why, there is action involved simply in staying alive – breathing, eating, sleeping . . .

'Also, my friend, leaving the battlefield and heading for the forest does not automatically guarantee that you will actually leave the war behind, don't you see? You will carry the war in your head and brood over whether you did the right thing by walking away. You will worry about your sons and brothers who are still fighting the war. You will die a thousand deaths as you beat yourself up over what you yourself will see as your betrayal.'

Arjuna could not deny, even to himself, the truth of Krishna's words. As usual, his friend had seen right through him. It was scary how Krishna seemed to know him better than he knew himself.

'Such a man,' continued Krishna, 'who believes he has "given up" action simply because he is not doing it, even though he is still attached to it in his head, is the worst kind of hypocrite. Do not be him, Arjuna.

'Be instead the man who does his duty sincerely, with no hope of reward. Be instead the man who treats his work as an offering to the gods, to the earth, to the Universe. Rest assured, the gods, the earth and the Universe will give you joy in return – generously, bountifully. And the eternal cycle of give and take between gods and men will be kept in motion.'

Arjuna nodded. This – the cycle of give and take between gods and men – he understood well. The gods had always made him work for his rewards, but whenever he had shown discipline, commitment and hard work, they had been unfailingly generous.

'If you only enjoy the gifts of the Universe,' said Krishna, 'the life-giving sun, the nourishing rain, the fertile earth, the lofty mountains, the flowing rivers – and not put your own shoulder to the wheel, offering your effort back to the Universe, you are no better than a common thief!

'But if you think of your work as an offering of gratitude, then your work will bring you joy; it will no longer seem a chore. I say to you, follow the example of the Universe. When the Universe gives us its gifts, it has absolutely nothing to gain in return, but it continues to give, to do what it is meant to, because if it didn't, the world would collapse into chaos. Do your own work in the same spirit, Arjuna, do it simply because it needs to be done, because if you don't, the world will collapse into chaos.'

Arjuna looked incredulously at Krishna. 'Surely you exaggerate, Krishna!' he said. 'Why will the world fall into chaos if I, just one man among the millions gathered here, walk away from this battlefield? How is it fair to me that, even though I realize what I am about to do is a sin, I still go ahead and do it, simply because you believe that the Universe will somehow be wrecked if I don't?'

'You are no ordinary man, Partha,' said Krishna, 'you are a leader of men. And for that reason, you have a responsibility to set the right example to the people who look up to you. Unfortunately, you don't have the luxury to do what you like - you have to think of what effect that will have on the people who follow you.'

'But wouldn't my walking away be a good example to them too?' pleaded Arjuna. 'Would they not see then, as I do, that this killing of brothers is wrong, that it will bring only sorrow, that all the riches in the world, if they are obtained at the cost of so much death and destruction, are worth no more than dust?'

Krishna smiled wistfully. 'Do you not wish that were so, my friend? But that's not the way it works. Ordinary men do not think like you – they believe that they are here on this earth to work, that work brings them the rewards they desire. Obviously, that makes them very attached to their work. The warriors of these two mighty armies are committed to the idea of their "work", which is fighting this war. If you walk away saying that you despise what they are about to do, you will be insulting them and their work. Worse, you will confuse them completely.

'Imagine if all leaders started doing this, walking away from their work because they felt that it was not making them happy. Imagine if they abandoned their responsibilities to their followers, people who trust them and believe in them, just because they feel that their own lives can be lived better. Would the world then not fall into chaos?'

IN WHICH KRISHNA WHIPS THE VEIL OFF TWO VILE VILLAINS

Arjuna was silent for a moment, digesting this. Krishna had a point there, but there was still something he didn't understand. 'But, Krishna, if I act the same way as ordinary, ignorant men, how does that make me any better than them?'

'Good question, Arjuna,' said Krishna. 'And once again, I tell you, it is the spirit in which you do your work that makes all the difference. The ignorant man believes that he himself is responsible for his actions and therefore has a right to rewards for those actions. When he doesn't get those expected rewards, he gets upset and angry. When he does get them, he is elated, believing he made it happen.'

The hero looked at his charioteer, a little bemused. If a man wasn't himself responsible for his actions, who was? What was Krishna getting at?

'The wise man, however, knows that it is not he, but his nature, that makes him do what he does,' said Krishna. 'He knows that his particular nature – thinker, doer, leader, follower – is something he is born with, not something he has chosen for himself. Therefore, he simply does, with great dedication, what comes naturally to him, expecting nothing in return except the completion of the work. He accepts the result of those actions with neither great joy nor great sorrow, because he knows that he really had nothing to do with the action in the first place.

'Know this, Arjuna – to do your own work, to follow your own nature – which, in your case, is being a warrior and a leader – even imperfectly, is much, much better than trying to do someone else's work, even if you do that perfectly. Better to die in the pursuit of your own duty, for there is great danger in neglecting your duty to do someone else's.'

Arjuna sat still, completely absorbed, letting the words wash over him.

'You see, Mahabahu, work itself is neither good nor bad. It just is. To love your work because it is enjoyable or because you believe it is the right thing to do, is just as bad as hating your work because it is distasteful or because you believe it is wrong. To be averse to something is just as bad as being attached to something. Anger (hate) and desire (love) are the two great enemies of the mind – they confuse you and prevent you from seeing clearly, just as dust covers a mirror and smoke hides a flame.

'So go forth, Partha, slay these two mighty foes, free yourself from your fever of delusion, and fight!'

Lessons from the Gita

5. Life is a roller coaster. You can't control it, but you can enjoy it.

Human life is one giant roller-coaster ride – every up is followed by a down, every down by the inevitable up. And just like on a real roller coaster, we have absolutely no control over the interval between the highs and lows, or the speed at which our roller coaster takes them, or even just how steep each climb and fall is.

The difference between a real roller coaster and life, though, is this – on a real roller coaster, you can just sit back and enjoy the ride; in the human-life roller coaster, each one of the passengers has a job to do. Some have what everyone believes are Very Important Jobs, some have what everyone believes are Really Pointless And Silly Jobs That Anyone Can Do. But no one, not even the guy who everyone believes has the Most Important Job Of All, can actually control the roller coaster in any way.

Our mistake is that we don't realize this. We don't understand that while we are on the roller coaster, we are seeing only a very tiny part of it and have no idea what is happening anywhere else on it. We actually believe that we are in charge, that we ourselves are causing the roller coaster to go up and down, that how well – or badly – we do our jobs will determine its route. We work madly to achieve the ups – coming first in class, winning that tennis tournament, becoming Class President – and are ecstatic when they happen.

But even though we continue working equally hard, sometimes the downs arrive, despite our best efforts – a third position in the next test, a shin fracture the day before the upcoming tournament, the sudden realization that someone else is actually more popular. Why do these downs happen despite everything that we do right? Because the route of the roller coaster, you see, is determined not by what we do, but by a whole bunch of other things.

So what does that mean? If everything that is going to happen to us is going to happen anyway – since the roller coaster's route has already been built into it – why bother with doing anything at all? Might as well sit back and not do a thing, right?

No.

See, what you do on the ginormous roller coaster – being a sincere student, a good friend, a dutiful son or daughter, a caring elder brother or sister – may seem like a very small, unimportant thing in the grand scheme of things, but it actually helps to make that ride better or less scary for your co-passengers, and more fun for yourself (how boring not to do anything at all!). Also, it is only because each of your co-passengers – your parents, your teachers, your friends – is doing his or her job that the ride is as smooth and safe as it is for you!

If you don't do your job because you think it is too boring or annoying or not fun enough, you are being lazy, irresponsible and selfish. If you neglect your job to do someone else's (like sneaking out of the house to play a cricket match because a member of the regular team did not turn up – when you really should be watching your younger brother, who is terrified of being alone at home), you would actually be putting your co-passengers at risk. (Maybe it is easier to understand how awful this kind of thing is if you put yourself in your little brother's place). Either way, if you don't do your job sincerely, you don't deserve to be on that fabulous ride at all. So, sadly, there's no getting around it – you gotta do what you gotta do. *But*, says the Gita, you must do your work without expecting any kind of reward for it.

For instance, don't expect to top the class just because you studied really hard, or get disappointed when you don't. In fact, according to the Gita, performing an action (studying) *because* you want a certain result (to come first) is completely flawed action; the right way is to study *simply because that is your work, your duty as a student.* Similarly, just because

you were there for your friend when she was upset about something (action), it is wrong to expect that she will be there for you when you are upset (result). You were there for her because you were doing your duty as a friend, that's all.

The trick, really, is:

1. To never perform your actions with an eye on their results – because you have control only over the former, not the latter.
2. To never neglect your duty, however distasteful it may seem at that time, because you owe it to the Universe.
3. To treat your work as your sacred duty. Offer your work up to the Universe, and whatever the Universe decides to give back to you, keep calm and carry on.

The Terrible Twins inside our heads

Somewhere in the Conversation that takes place in the third chapter of the Gita, Arjuna asks Krishna, 'You know, Krishna, sometimes men do terrible, sinful things, even though they know it is wrong. It is as if an unstoppable force is making them do it, almost against their will. What is this force, do you know?' Here is Krishna's answer, identifying the twin ogres – Kama (desire) and Krodha (anger) – that we should all beware of.

श्रीभगवानुवाच ।
काम एष क्रोध एष रजोगुणसमुद्भवः ।
महाशनो महापाप्मा विद्ध्येनमिह वैरिणम् ॥३-३७॥

Shri Bhagavaan uvaacha
Kaama esha krodha esha rajo-guna-samudravaha
Mahaashano mahaapaapma viddhyenamiha vairinam

The Blessed Lord said:
This is desire, this is wrath, born of Rajas or passion.
It devours everything, it is most sinful. This is the
enemy – know it. (3-37)

What's in a name? Plenty!

You must have noticed that through the Gita conversation, Krishna and Arjuna address each other by a whole bunch of different names. All the names are appropriate, and mean something special about each of them. Plus, they break the monotony of using the same names in a 700-shloka conversation between the same two people. And of course, they sound grand and adoring and affectionate in turn, and add a touch of music and poetry to the epic text.

Here is a selection of our two protagonists' many names as used in the Gita, with their meanings.

Arjuna's names for Krishna:

- **Achyuta:** One who never falls from his high and noble position
- **Madhusudana:** Slayer of the demon Madhu
- **Madhava:** Another name for Vishnu (whose avatar Krishna is), who is called Madhava because he is the husband of the goddess Madhavi, or Lakshmi
- **Purushottama:** Best among men
- **Janardhana:** The one who destroys ignorance
- **Hrishikesha:** Master of the senses
- **Varshneya:** Descendant of Vrishni, a king who started the Vrishni dynasty
- **Ananta:** The limitless one
- **Aprameya**: The immeasurable one
- **Vishwaroopa:** The one whose form is the Universe itself
- **Devadeva:** God of gods
- **Sakha:** Dear friend

Krishna's names for Arjuna:

- **Partha:** Son of Pritha, which is another name for Kunti
- **Dhananjaya:** Conqueror of wealth
- **Mahabahu:** The mighty-armed one
- **Gudakesha:** One who has conquered sleep (it is believed that Arjuna could go for days on end without sleep)

- **Kaunteya:** Son of Kunti
- **Bharatarshabha:** Best of the Bharatas
- **Parantapa:** Foe-conqueror
- **Kurusattama:** Best of the Kurus
- **Dhanurdhara:** He who carries the bow
- **Kapidhvaja:** He who has a monkey on his flag (Arjuna's ensign in war featured none other than Hanuman)
- **Savyasachi:** The ambidextrous archer
- **Sakha:** Dear friend

'And the Blessed Lord said to Arjuna,' went on Sanjaya, ' "This secret of happiness – of doing your work honestly, whatever that work may be, expecting nothing in return – is nothing new. I have revealed this very truth to many in the past – to Vivasvan, for one, who passed it on to his son Manu, who passed it on to his son Ikshvaku, who passed it further down the line. But the truth tends to get changed or lost as it passes from man to man, from generation to generation, and it needs to be retold ever so often. And that is why I reveal this truth to you again, Arjuna, because you trust me and because you are my friend."'

In the Throne Room at Hastinapura, King Dhritarashtra did a double take. Manu and Ikshvaku were the forefathers of Prince Rama of Ayodhya, kings of the ancient past, who had passed thousands of years ago. How could Krishna have told them anything?

८

the yoga of knowledge ⋯⋯◄◄◆►►⋯⋯ gyana yoga

IN WHICH KRISHNA REVEALS THAT HE IS A LITTLE UNUSUAL

On the battlefield of Kurukshetra, Arjuna was no less startled at Krishna's words. 'What?' he sputtered. 'How could you have told Vivasvan anything? I know we are no longer young men, Krishna, but there is no way you could have been around when Vivasvan was!'

Krishna took a deep breath. What he was about to say was not something he expected Arjuna to swallow easily, never mind that it was the truth. Bracing himself for complete disbelief from his friend, Krishna plunged in.

'I have lived many lives before this one, Arjuna, and so have you. The difference is that I remember what all those lives were, and you don't. I don't need to be born as a human on earth, Partha, for I am the Lord of all Creatures, who is never born and will never die. But,' Krishna went on, 'I *choose*, time and again, to take birth on earth.'

Arjuna stared, uncomprehending. Lord of all Creatures? What in heaven's name could his friend mean?

But Krishna was speaking again. The familiar, beloved voice had a different tone and timbre to it now; it sounded almost other-worldly to Arjuna's suddenly hyper-attentive ears.

'Whenever righteousness dips and unrighteousness begins to rule the roost, O Bharata, I send forth myself. To protect the good, to destroy the sins of the bad and to make sure righteousness returns to the land, I come into being, in age after age.

'Men who understand this truth about me fly joyfully from fear, desire and anger to find a safe harbour in me. The blazing white heat of this wisdom burns away their doubts and sets them free. They never need to be born again, to suffer. Because, you see, Partha,' Krishna smiled, 'such men *become* me.'

Lessons from the Gita

6. Go(o)d will find a way.

So is Krishna really God? According to the Gita, and according to the Hindus, absolutely! And does this God keep coming back to earth, in different incarnations or avatars, to restore order and goodness to society, whenever unrighteousness overtakes the world? Without a doubt, says the Gita.

You may or may not believe that Krishna is God, or that God comes down to earth regularly to protect the good. You may believe in a different God, or you may believe in a hero who does similar things – protects the good, destroys the bad, re-establishes order in society and inspires others to live good lives themselves. Mahatma Gandhi, for example. Or Batman.

Either way, though, you most likely believe in Good (which, most God-believing people will agree, is another name for God). Even though the world around us often seems packed with selfish, angry and hateful people, most of us find it easier to admire, respect and love someone who is good and kind and unselfish. Even though the bad guys seem to prosper – they seem to be more successful and more powerful than the good guys – most of us would rather imitate the good guys. If only because, from our own personal experiences, we know that while it is often easier to be bad, we are happier and more at peace when we've been good.

It isn't always easy to know *what* is 'good', though. People who believe in God read books that carry what they believe is the word of God, and follow their suggestions. Many people who don't believe in God also use these books to help them know what the right way to live is – the only difference is that they believe these words come from wise men and women, not from someone called God. Others just try to be like people who they believe are good people.

You can do it too. Make a list of all the people that you think are good people. Your list could include anyone from great leaders such as Martin Luther King Jr, who fought injustice not with anger and weapons but with grace and non-violence, to the vegetable-seller down the road, who never forgets to smile at you even though her arthritic knees are killing her. Next to each name, write down one or two qualities that you admire about that person, and that you would like to emulate in your own life.

Then start trying to actually follow their example. Every time you get really mad at someone for treating you wrong, or feel like snapping at someone because you are upset about something else, pause for a moment. Take several deep breaths, count to ten, punch a pillow – whatever works for you – and then think about what the people on your list would have done in a similar situation. Do the same.

The Hindus believe that God isn't someone or something that lives outside of us. God, they say, lives within us – all we have to do is to connect with Him. When we do (as Krishna said to Arjuna), we actually *become* Him. When you follow the example of good people, you are connecting to the Good that lives inside you. By and by, if you work very hard, you will *become* it. Why, you may even start making it to other people's 'good people' lists (although *that's* not why you should be good)!

Stretch that a bit, and you could think of inspiring leaders as avatars – small gods in human form, appearing in every age when unrighteousness is rampant, leading all of us towards the light of truth and justice. Not as far-fetched as it seems, is it?

The ten avatars of Vishnu

Hindus believe that Lord Vishnu has come down to earth nine times in the past to keep His promise to mankind – 'Whenever there is a rise in unrighteousness, I will send forth myself to destroy it and restore order'. We are still waiting for Him to appear in our age – He is supposed to arrive as Kalki the horseman, brandishing a blazing sword – but these are the avatars that have gone before.

First, he came down as a

1. **Giant Fish**, **Matsya**; then, the
2. **Giant Sea Turtle**, **Kurma**; followed by the
3. **Giant Boar**, **Varaha**; after which came the

4. **Fierce Man-Lion**, **Narasimha**; on the heels of whom arrived the
5. **Dwarf Priest**, **Vamana**; who made way for the blood and gore of the
6. **Angry Young Axeman**, **Parashurama**; after which – *phew!* – was the turn of the
7. **Righteous King and hero of the Ramayana**, **Rama**; followed by our hero, the
8. **Flute-playing prankster, the darling of all maidens, and Arjuna's BFF**, **Krishna**; and finally, the
9. **Royal Sage**, Siddhartha Gautama the Buddha.

It may seem like an odd and completely random set of animals and men, but the cool part is, it may not be! Theories abound about why exactly these animals were chosen as avatars, and why they appeared in that order. Here's one of them.

The order of the 10 avatars (or the Dashavatara), says the theory, actually holds the secret to the evolution of man. It is now a widely accepted scientific fact that life began in the water, but the Hindu sages knew of it, apparently, many millennia ago, which is why the first avatar is a Fish!

Then comes the sea turtle, or the Amphibian. After which comes the boar, the Mammal. The Man-Lion follows – this creature is almost a man, similar to the next branch in the tree of evolution, the Great Apes. The dwarf who comes next is a nod to the short-statured Early Man, who is followed by the true *Homo sapiens sapiens*, Parashurama.

Now it begins to get really interesting. Note that Parashurama's weapon of choice was an axe, which, according to this theory, indicates the beginning of the Iron Age, and the end of the age of hunting and gathering as man began to use iron implements like the plough. Parashurama is followed by King Rama – the fact that he is a king tells us we are now in the age of settled cities and centralized administration.

He is followed by Krishna, who is a symbol of culture (music, dance) and leisure (prank-playing). Culture and leisure were only possible once man was settled in an agricultural community with a king who maintained law and order – no longer was he anxious about his safety, or where his next meal was coming from; he now had enough time and opportunity to explore his playful and creative side.

After Krishna came the Buddha, who symbolizes the next stage in human development – detachment from worldly attractions and the quest for answers to the real meaning of life. Which, logically, happened only after man had discovered that all the things money and power and fame could buy did not make him truly, madly, deeply happy.

Very cool, right? You can ask around for other theories, or come up with your own different ones to explain this particular sequence of avatars.

P.S. *Although these 10 avatars are the most popular, several ancient texts tell us there were at least 14 more, to make 24 in all. This list ends, as the Dashavatara list does, with Kalki, but begins not with Matsya but with Adi Purusha, the first man of creation. The list also includes Rishabha, the first Tirthankara (whose followers are called the Jains); the enchantress Mohini, who denied the Asuras their share of the golden nectar of immortality after the Churning of the Ocean; Dhanvantari, the patron saint of Indian medicine; Krishna's brother Balarama; and – hold your breath! – our old friend Sage Vyasa himself!*

Here's a last bit of trivia – in some Hindu traditions, Krishna is not considered an avatar of Vishnu. How can Krishna be a mere avatar, they argue, when he says so clearly in the Gita that it is He Himself who is the Supreme One? Every other avatar in the Dashavatara list, they insist, is, therefore, an avatar of Krishna, not Vishnu! How do they deal with the now-empty slot at Avatar No. 8? Simple. They insert Balarama there.

IN WHICH ARJUNA LEARNS THAT EXERCISE IS A VALID FORM OF WORSHIP

Arjuna stared at Krishna, speechless. A feeling of déjà vu stirred somewhere in the depths of his mind. 'You have always known that Krishna is the Lord Incarnate,' a voice whispered, 'but you always forget. You have always known that you are Nara, the human half of God, and that he is Narayana, the divine half of man, which is what makes you both so inseparable.'

Arjuna started guiltily. If Krishna was really God, and he had known it, he really should have been treating him with a lot more devotion, a lot more respect. Instead, he had been disagreeing with him, arguing with him, asking him to explain himself . . . What was *wrong* with him?

'Don't be so hard on yourself,' said the voice soothingly, 'It is Krishna himself who makes you forget, so that you are not overwhelmed by his glory, so that you can be his friend. That's how much he loves you.'

The voice faded away. Arjuna tried to recall what it had said, because something told him it was desperately important, but strangely, no matter how hard he tried, he could not remember a single word.

Shaking his head irritably, Arjuna forced himself to focus.

'Men take different roads to come to me, Arjuna,' Krishna was saying, 'and I accept all of them. Whatever work each may do – whether it is scholarly study and meditation, which the thinkers do, whether it is raising arms against injustice like the men of action do, whether it is doing business like the traders, whether it is tilling the fields and taking care of the cattle as the farmers and cowherds do – the work itself does not affect me, and I accept it all in the same spirit, as long as the action is right.'

'But what is "right" action, Krishna? How will I know if my action is right?'

'I've said it before, Arjuna, and I say it again to you: If you perform your action simply because it needs to be done, without desire for reward, without fear of consequence, if you offer your action to me as a sacrifice, if you are free of jealousy when you act, if you remain the same whether your action brings you success or failure, that is right action, whatever that action may be.'

Arjuna shook his head, puzzled. 'Offer my action as a sacrifice? What does that even mean, Krishna?'

'Different people offer different actions to me as a sacrifice,' said Krishna. 'Some withdraw from the world – they shut their eyes and ears, and sacrifice the pleasures of the senses. Some embrace the world – they see everything around them as a gift of the Universe and enjoy it in the right spirit, claiming nothing for themselves – that is their sacrifice. Others fast, sacrificing their hunger; or exercise, sacrificing their comfort. Still others practise breath control, sacrificing their most important life force, the breath itself. And then there are some who offer a combination of all these to discipline their bodies and control their minds.

'All these people practise self-discipline and sacrifice; that is how they worship me, and I accept it all. They understand that true sacrifice does not mean the offering of things – money, possessions, gold – but the offering of themselves – their pleasure, their pain, their desire, their anger. They have complete faith in me, in the idea that self-discipline brings true wisdom, which brings in its wake true happiness.

'But he who offers no sacrifice at all,' Krishna went on, his voice growing stern, 'who does not believe in anything, who practises no self-control but does exactly what he likes at all times, there is no wisdom for him, and therefore no happiness, in this world or any other.'

Arjuna nodded. Discipline was the soldier's credo, and no one knew better than he just how vital it was to victory. But did it bring wisdom? Or happiness? He wasn't so sure.

'So I say to you, Dhananjaya,' said Krishna, 'have faith in the rightness of the action you are about to perform. Sacrifice your doubts and your grief to me. Know that it is your inaction, and not your action, that will make you a sinner.

'Stand up, O Bharata, and draw your bowstring!'

Lessons from the Gita

7. Keep the faith. The rest will follow.*

If you think about it, anyone who has achieved anything in this world has done so because she had faith, because she believed – in an idea, in God, in herself, or in all of them.

Madame Curie believed implicitly that even though a mineral called pitchblende was mostly made up of uranium, there was a tiny amount of something else in there too. It took her 15 years of tireless work, which included grinding down about a ton of pitchblende, to figure out how to separate the 'something else' – which she named Radium – and prove to the world that her hunch had been right.

Young Albanian nun Sister Teresa was headmistress in a school in Kolkata where she had worked for 20 years when she got 'the call within the call' – God, she would say later, had ordered her to leave the convent and help the poor while living among them. She followed the order, even though she was plagued by doubt about her decision and was even reduced to begging for food in the first year. She went on to start the Missionaries of Charity, whose mission was to serve the 'poorest of the poor'. Thirty years later, the world recognized her years of selfless service to the poor by awarding her the Nobel Peace Prize.

*Terms and conditions apply.

More recently, author Joanne K. (you know, J.K.) Rowling believed so much that children would enjoy her story about a boy wizard that she never stopped sending it out to publishers. Seventeen publishers returned the manuscript, saying they didn't think it was good enough. The eighteenth one agreed to take a chance on her. Today, Harry Potter is one of the most famous and popular fictional characters in the world.

Of course, just having faith isn't enough. You should also be prepared to back the faith up with tons of hard work. You need to be able to make all the sacrifices it takes, and yes, you need to be able to do your work 'with no expectation of reward'. If you think you want to be a writer someday, for instance, you will have to write, and write, and write, always focusing on the job at hand, but never neglecting your primary duty as a student, which is working at your lessons.

Such an effort will need everything that Krishna says it will – self-discipline (it is so much easier to watch TV when you have a free afternoon than to sit down and write something), many sacrifices (if you haven't done your quota of writing for the week, you will have to be prepared to skip that movie you had planned with your friends or wake up really early on Sunday morning to finish the writing), and, of course, a lot of faith.

If you manage to do all that, though, wisdom is guaranteed. Maybe you will realize, after six months of being super-disciplined about writing, that writing isn't for you. Maybe you will discover how much you love it and become even surer that that's what you want to do in life. Either way, never again will you have to wonder whether writing is for you or not, no matter what anyone says. In other words, there is no more doubt, or fear. And if that isn't a recipe for happiness, what is?

If we had to put it down as a mathematical equation, it would look something like this:

Faith + Self-discipline* = Wisdom → Happiness**

*Self-discipline = Sacrifice + Hard Work

** Happiness = No Doubts + No Fear

He is a silent guardian, a watchful protector, a dark knight

One of the most powerful – and comforting – pair of shlokas in the Gita is Krishna's promise to Arjuna, and through him, to all humanity, that he will incarnate himself on earth whenever, wherever, unrighteousness begins to take over. Here they are in the original Sanskrit for you to enjoy.

Remember this is great literature in one of the oldest languages in the world, so try saying the shlokas out loud – go on, don't be shy! – to really enjoy their beauty and power.

यदा यदा हि धर्मस्य ग्लानिर्भवति भारत ।
अभ्युत्थानमधर्मस्य तदात्मानं सृजाम्यहम् ॥४-७॥

yadaa yadaa hi dharmasya glaanirbhavati bhaarata
abhyutthaanam-adharmasya tadaatmaanam
srijaamyaham

Whenever there is a decline of righteousness and rise of unrighteousness, O Bharata, then I send forth Myself. (4-7)

परित्राणाय साधूनां विनाशाय च दुष्कृताम् ।
धर्मसंस्थापनार्थाय सम्भवामि युगे युगे ॥४-८॥

paritraanaaya saadhoonaam vinaashaaya cha
dushkritaam
dharma-sansthaa-panaar-thaaya sambhavaami
yugey yugey

To protect the good, to destroy the wicked and to establish righteousness, I will return, from age to age. (4-8)

4

the yoga of renunciation of action ····◄◄◄◆►►►···· karma sanyasa yoga

IN WHICH KRISHNA PLUGS ANOTHER LOOPHOLE

'I am still confused, Krishna,' said Arjuna. 'You say, so emphatically, that sacrifice is the first step towards wisdom and happiness. Wouldn't it be better for me, then, to sacrifice this war, give up the power and glory that would be mine if I won, and walk away? But you also say, equally firmly, that doing the work you are meant to do, unselfishly, is the way to wisdom and happiness. I don't know which path to choose. Don't give me options, Krishna. Just tell me, once and for all, which is the better of the two.'

'Listen then, Partha, and listen well,' said Krishna. 'Both the path of sacrifice and renunciation, and the path of doing your work unselfishly, lead to wisdom and happiness. But of the two, the path of unselfish work is better than the path of renunciation.'

Arjuna stared. There it was, then. Krishna had stated it as directly as was possible. But how could that be true? He had always been taught to believe that the way of the sadhus and rishis, who sacrificed worldly pleasures and spent their entire lives in meditation, was superior to every other path. He leaned in to listen to Krishna elaborate.

'For you see, Mahabahu, he who does his work without loving it or hating it, he who neither desires something from his work nor rejects anything about it, *is* a man who has sacrificed everything, renounced everything. Only those who do not truly understand this would say that action – doing what the world requires of you – is somehow inferior to withdrawing from the world. The wise see clearly that the ways of renunciation and action are actually the same.'

With alacrity, Arjuna seized on the last sentence that Krishna had spoken. At last – a loophole that could potentially help him escape the war! Even better, this loophole had Krishna's approval – the only endorsement that mattered to him. 'So, Krishna,' he said eagerly, 'if renunciation and action are the same, what if I chose renunciation, and left the battlefield? Maybe right action is *better*, but you've just said that the path of renunciation also leads to God, so let me walk that path.'

Krishna smiled. 'Alas, Mahabahu, renunciation does not mean walking away from action. That would count as "inaction", which is a *rejection* of action. And rejection is an action too, and a selfish one at that, so you are achieving neither renunciation nor right action when you walk away. This kind of inaction is not noble – it is lazy, cowardly, irresponsible. The challenge, you see, is to strive for inaction *while being fully involved in action*. In other words, the challenge is to strive not only for right action but right *inaction*.'

'Right inaction? What does that mean? You are befuddling my poor mind even more than it is already, Krishna, you are teasing me.'

'I wish I were, Partha, but this is the honest and supreme truth. Blessed is the man who is able to be completely involved in action with his body and his senses, while being completely steeped in inaction at his core. This man's Atman is always still, undisturbed, unattached to the actions of his body and his senses. It neither expects rewards from his action, not fears the results of his action. It is neither attached to action nor does it reject action. *That* is right inaction, Arjuna, not what you propose to do.'

Arjuna frowned. The mists in his mind were beginning to clear somewhat, and a glimmer of understanding was beginning to shine through. But oh, how hard it was going to be to detach his core from the heinous acts that his limbs were about to commit!

Lessons from the Gita

8. Yup, responsibility is a heavy burden. Now shush up and shoulder it.

Responsibility is a big word. And it is not quite the same thing as duty. Duty is an obligation, something that you *have* to do, which you could be punished for not doing. But responsibility is an option – there is no rule that says you have to take it, and no one can punish you for not taking it. But, according to the Gita, and according to any good person's code of living, your responsibility, however unpleasant it may be, is just as sacred as your duty.

As a student, doing your lessons is your *duty*. Being respectful to your teachers is your duty. Getting to school on time is your duty.

Now, let's say you are a maths whiz, and you have promised a student who is weak at the subject that you will help him with his maths lessons after school. Keeping your promise becomes your *responsibility*. As a member of the school community, making sure you intervene when a classmate is bullying someone else, even if the bully is your closest friend, is your responsibility. As a school prefect, being a role model to every other student – by being punctual, disciplined, regular with your schoolwork, respectful of the school's rules, even when you are sure no one is watching – is your responsibility.

Duties could be unpleasant, but we usually end up doing them because of the fear of reprimand. Since responsibilities have no such fear factor attached to them, we try to shuck them off, especially when we know they could be unpleasant. Standing up to a close friend X, for instance, because you don't approve of her talking badly about a common friend, Y, to someone else, is a very unpleasant responsibility, so we reject it. Then, because we feel guilty about not doing what we know was right, we find a hundred reasons to excuse ourselves: 'It's not my problem.'; 'Oh, that's between X and Y, so who am I to interfere?'; 'I don't want to make a fuss.'; 'I don't want to hurt X.'; 'X is too important to me – I can't risk losing her by bringing this up.'; 'Now that I know what X is like, I'm going to hang out with her much less – I'm sure she'll get the message.'

The trouble with these excuses is that that this exactly what they are – excuses. The trouble is that you slowly begin to believe that they are the truth. The trouble is that letting yourself off the hook for responsibilities that you should have fulfilled but didn't, becomes a habit. The trouble is that 'It's not my problem' could end up becoming your motto for life. And that would be a shame.

You wouldn't want to grow up into that adult who saw someone bleeding on the side of the road after an accident but sped away because she told herself, 'It's not my problem'. You would not want to become the business baron who knew that one of his best customers was employing children in his factories but overlooked it because he told himself, 'It's not my problem'. You would not want to be the homemaker who knew that her cook was having a hard time with her

alcoholic husband at home but still expected her to turn up exactly on time each day because 'what happens in her house is not my problem.'

Of course, in the Mahabharata, Arjuna is in a far tougher situation than most of us will ever be. It is his responsibility as a leader, a warrior and a good, righteous person, to stand up to unrighteousness and to protect the people of the land from selfish, grasping, unethical people, but he will have to kill his closest family to achieve that. But responsibilities, according to the Gita, are sacred.

And that's why Krishna will not let Arjuna escape his terrible responsibility. And that's why Arjuna continues to listen to what his friend is saying, even though he does not like what he hears, because in his heart, he knows, as do we, that Krishna is right.

IN WHICH KRISHNA DESCRIBES THE HAPPY MAN – AGAIN

'You know this, Kaunteya,' said Krishna, 'but I will tell you once again. Both the pain as well as the pleasure that come to you from objects that appeal to your senses are, without exception, sources of sorrow. They have a beginning, and they have an end. The wise man understands this – he neither rejoices when something pleasant happens nor grieves when something unpleasant does.

'Imagine the happiness that such a man enjoys even when he lives on earth, Partha! All his joy springs from within himself, not from anything on the outside. He is never attracted to the wondrous things the world throws at him, because he has his senses under control. He is never confused or bewildered, because he has his mind under control. He is able to look beyond the obvious; outer appearances do not fool him. He sees me in all creatures – in a learned and gentle priest, a cow, an elephant, a dog, or a an outcaste – and treats them all just the same, just as I do. He offers his work as a sacrifice to me, knowing that I am the Enjoyer of Sacrifices; he sees me everywhere, in everything, knowing that I am the Lord of all the Worlds; he trusts me completely, knowing that I am the Friend of all Beings; and he is at peace.'

Everyone's the same on the inside

विद्याविनयसंपन्ने ब्राह्मणे गवि हस्तिनि ।
शुनि चैव श्वपाके च पण्डिताः समदर्शिनः ॥५-१८॥

vidyaa-vinaya-sampanne braahmane gavi hastini
shuni chaiva shvapaake cha panditaah
samadarshinaha

Sages see with an equal eye, a learned and humble Brahmin, a cow, an elephant, a dog, or an outcaste.
(5-18)

Most religions in the world preach some version of this truth – that all creatures are equal and that they should all therefore be treated equally. Which is why it is so surprising that so few of us follow this excellent advice. Never mind other creatures, we don't even treat all humans the same; we treat the rich differently from the poor, the beautiful differently from the not-so-beautiful, the powerful very differently from the powerless, and those who we serve very differently from those who serve us.

Read the shloka out loud – to yourself, to your family, to your friends, to remind yourself and them of this one vital step on the journey to a good and happy life.

Echoes of the Gita

Writers, artists, musicians and film-makers often take on the role of being the conscience of society. Through their work, they point out uncomfortable truths, make people think, and initiate change in mindsets.

Two of the most beloved singer-songwriters of the 20th century – Paul McCartney and Michael Jackson – had their own unique ways of conveying the message that the Gita does in this chapter.

In his song, 'Ebony and Ivory', Paul McCartney wondered poignantly why people with differently coloured skins (or who look different from one another, or come from different countries, or follow different religions) on the outside, cannot seem to live in friendship with one another, when the black and white keys on his piano keyboard do so with such perfect harmony, producing beautiful music together. A generation later, in his similarly titled song 'Black or White', Michael Jackson urged his listeners to understand that it wasn't colour or race that made people different from one another, but what they were like in their hearts and minds. Once you understood that, he said, anyone could become your brother (or sister) – it really wouldn't matter if they were black or white. Hard to disagree with either of these guys, right?

६

the yoga of meditation ⋯⋯◄◄◄◆►►►⋯⋯ dhyana yoga

IN WHICH KRISHNA EXPLAINS THE IMPORTANCE OF ME-TIME

'You imagine, Arjuna,' said Krishna, 'that walking away from the battlefield makes you a sanyasi, a monk, on the same level as those who have walked away from worldly pleasures. But I say to you, my friend, shunning the action you are supposed to do does not make you a monk. A true sanyasi is one who fulfils his responsibilities without craving for rewards, without fearing punishment.

'You know well, Partha, that such a state of mind is not easy to achieve. But believe it or not, there are simple, practical steps to start off on that journey, which *anyone* can follow.'

There he goes again, thought Arjuna, shaking his head in admiration, breaking down a complex task into a series of logical, sequential actions.

'It is really all about disciplined action, or yoga,' explained Krishna. 'Getting to monkhood by doing the work you are meant to do in a disciplined, detached fashion is Karma Yoga, or the Yoga of Action; we have already talked about this. Getting to wisdom through quiet contemplation and scholarly study is Gyana Yoga, or the Yoga of Knowledge. A third kind of yoga is Dhyana Yoga, the Yoga of Meditation, which can be practised both by the Karma Yogis – the doers, and the Gyana Yogis – the thinkers.'

Arjuna leaned forward, curious. That was interesting, that there was a yoga that straddled both the thinker-zone and the doer-zone. Interesting, because he wasn't quite sure in which zone he was, at the moment. Krishna insisted he was a doer, but the thinker route sounded so much more appealing just now.

'Here are the basic steps of the yoga of meditation,' said Krishna, and proceeded to list them out.

1. First, the yogi (the person doing the yoga) must try to empty his mind of all thought, to rein in his senses.
2. It is important for him to be alone, away from people and other distractions, so that he is able to focus better on the task at hand.
3. For his meditation, he should find a clean, quiet place and a firm, flat seat, at a comfortable height, which he must cover with sacred grass, a deerskin and a clean cloth.
4. Holding his body, neck and head erect and still, he should focus his gaze on the tip of his nose, and not look anywhere else.

5. Then, serene and fearless, his mind and senses under control, he should concentrate single-mindedly on his innermost soul, on me.
6. This he should do, not once, not twice, but over and over again, regularly, with fierce determination, without slacking, even though it is difficult – for it is only through relentless practice, through doing something over and over again, that one learns to do that thing well.

'Remember, Partha, that if yoga has to work, the yogi has to take care of his body well. Yoga is neither for him who eats too much nor for him who eats too little, neither for him who sleeps too much nor for him who sleeps too little. But the man who does everything in moderation – who is moderate in his eating, moderate in his activities, moderate in recreation, moderate in both sleep and wakefulness – he will find that the yoga of meditation will take away his unhappiness and give him the joy he is seeking.

'You do understand, Kaunteya, that it will not happen all at once. But if the yogi is regular and disciplined about his yoga, he cannot help but gain, little by little, the tranquillity he desires. Of course his mind will wander away from time to time – that is its nature – but he should pull it back, restrain it, each time, and not be lazy.'

Arjuna smiled wryly. That was easier said than done.

'Through the practice of yoga, the yogi becomes like a lamp in a windless place,' Krishna continued, 'whose flame does not flicker but burns bright and tall and true. His senses, which he has disciplined, stop scattering at the slightest provocation. His mind, which he has learnt to control, does not flit restlessly from one thought to another, but stays calm and still. Only when the mind is still, Partha, and the passions are at rest, can the yogi experience the infinite joy that lives within him, the great happiness that is beyond the reach of his senses but always within reach of his heart. The greatest sorrow will not touch him once he has experienced this joy; no other reward will he ever desire.

'When this has been achieved, the scales fall away from his eyes. The chains that bind him to the world drop from him, and he sees the world as it really is. In everything around him he sees a bit of himself, and in himself, he sees a bit of everything around him. In the clear light of wisdom, he is able to look beyond the differences on the outside to the sameness on the inside. He sees that he is one with the world, equal to every other creature, no different from any of them. To him, a clod of earth is no different from a piece of gold, and a friend is no different from a foe.'

It seemed incredible, thought Arjuna, that a man could reach such a state of peace and stillness – his own mind, at the moment, was tossing about like a rowboat in a stormy sea.

'As you might expect, Arjuna, this perfect yogi also sees me in everything and everything in me. I am always within his sights; I am never lost to him. And he therefore is never lost to me.'

Lessons from the Gita

9. Self-discipline is like a muscle. Exercise it regularly to stay in great emotional shape.

There can be no debate about it – self-discipline is at the root of a happy, healthy, stress-free life. And we're not even talking exercise or meditation here, just basic self-discipline, like watching no more than half an hour of television on a school night, or brushing your teeth before you go to bed, or not finishing the entire pack of potato chips at one go.

Just like responsibility, self-discipline is not something anyone else can impose on you, but something you impose on yourself, because you can see, plain as daylight, what its benefits are – which, in the examples here, are having enough time left over to go out and play *and* do your homework (happiness), saving yourself some scary trips to the dentist (no-stress-ness) and holding space in your stomach for something more nutritious (health), respectively.

Children who make it a habit to pack their school bags the night before, grow up to become tweens who make time to practise their music every day, who grow up to become teens who refuse to bunk school just because a friend throws them a dare, who grow up to become college students who will never drink and drive, who grow up to become adults who exercise regularly and eat right and do well at their jobs and make time for their families. Do you see a pattern here? Do you see that self-discipline is a habit, not something you are born with, which means it can be cultivated, by anyone? Do you see how it gets easier and easier the more you do it, and the earlier you start?

When its benefits are so obvious, why do so few of us exercise self-discipline? Because, for one thing, there is no immediate repercussion (your teeth will not fall out by the next morning if you don't brush your teeth one night). Very often, the repercussion isn't even guaranteed, there is only a high risk of it (you could get suspended if you are caught bunking school, but not everyone who bunks gets caught).

However, the reason most of us don't live a disciplined life, even though we really want to, is because it is notoriously hard to do it. In the Gita, Krishna himself acknowledges how difficult it is. Luckily, he also offers a simple method to get started on the journey towards a disciplined life. It requires no fancy props, no special setting, no prep before, no cleaning up after. It doesn't even require you to give up television or candy. Feels like it is worth a shot?

Great! All you need to do is carve out fifteen minutes each day to sit down by yourself. Make sure you are in a quiet, clean place and on a comfortable seat (the deerskin covering that Krishna mentions is not mandatory). Posture is important – don't slouch. Close your eyes to shut out distractions and focus on something. In the Gita, Krishna asks you to focus on the tip of your nose. Yoga teachers may tell you to imagine a flame burning between your eyebrows and focus on that. You could even keep your eyes open and pick one object in the room to focus on (but hey, this one object cannot be the TV, iPad or phone – gotcha!).

Now comes the hardest part – controlling your thoughts. The easiest way to do this is to think only about one thing. For instance, five things that happened in the last twenty-four hours that you are grateful for. Stuff you could have done better today (or yesterday, depending on what time of day you sit down to do this). Stuff that made you mad or sad over the last week – and why.

Does that sound simple enough? The important thing, however, is to do it every single day, preferably at the same time, until it becomes a habit. Do it for two weeks, and see how proud it makes you that you could challenge yourself to do something and actually do it. Then, slowly start adding other routines to this one – the junk-food-only-on-weekends routine, the tidying-up-your-desk-twice-a-week routine, the reading-four-new-books-a-month routine. Your self-esteem will zoom, you will become fearless about taking on tough challenges and you will be a more confident, much happier person.

What's not to like about that?

IN WHICH ARJUNA LEARNS THAT JUST TRYING TO BE GOOD CAN WIN YOU BROWNIE POINTS IN YOUR NEXT LIFE

Arjuna shook his head. 'Easy for you to talk, Krishna,' he said gloomily, 'but the mind is restless, fickle, so easily distracted. It is a slave to the senses, and obstinate with desire. How can one ever succeed in taming it? You might as well try and tame the wind!'

'Without doubt, Mahabahu, the mind is inordinately difficult to control,' said Krishna. 'But don't lose heart, Kaunteya, for it can be done. Relentless practice and non-attachment will see you through. I agree that yoga of any kind is hard to attain for the man who has no self-control, but for the man who practises self-control in every aspect of his life, it is really not so difficult if he makes the effort, the right kind of effort. Trust me on this.'

But Arjuna was not convinced. 'Tell me this, Krishna. Let's say I really, *really* want to reach this state of bliss, of complete non-attachment, and that I try as hard as I can to get there. But what if I fail? What if my mind wanders away like a wayward cloud? What happens to me then? I will not have achieved happiness on earth, but nor will I be accepted in heaven. I fear that will be my fate, Krishna. Is there any point even starting on such a difficult path when reaching the destination is such a remote possibility?'

'Oh Partha, do not trouble your mind about this,' said Krishna. 'I assure you, dear friend, that no such fate awaits him who tries and fails. Neither in this life, nor in the next, will such a man walk the path of sorrow. When this man is born again, the merit he has gained from his practice of yoga in his previous lifetime, however imperfect that yoga might have been, will ensure that he starts with an advantage in his new life. He will be born in a house of yogis, pure-minded people like himself, and he will progress further along the path to becoming the perfect yogi.

'Listen well, Kurunandana. The true yogi – the man who does his work in a disciplined manner and fulfils his responsibilities without being attached to the fruits of his actions – he is greater than the sanyasi who leaves the world behind; he is greater than the man who performs rituals without fail; he is greater than the man of knowledge.

'So be a yogi, Arjuna. With a heart full of faith and devotion and love for me, my dearest friend, shoulder your bow. The time for action is here.'

Mind-Monkey, Will-Horse

In the 34th shloka of this chapter, Arjuna compares the restless mind to the wind and wonders how it can ever be tamed. Other books of wisdom express similar thoughts. In Buddhist and Chinese philosophy, a phrase often used to describe this is 'mind-monkey, will-horse'. It compares the mind to a monkey that leaps constantly from branch to branch in a forest, never still, never happy with the fruit it has in its hand, always looking for better fruit; and the will to a horse, always galloping away in whatever direction it fancies, so difficult to rein in. Just like Krishna in the Gita, the Buddha also reckoned that controlling the mind-monkey and the will-horse is the way to Nirvana, or ultimate happiness.

Here is Arjuna's lament about the mind, in the original Sanskrit, for you to enjoy.

चञ्चलं हि मनः कृष्ण प्रमाथि बलवद्दृढम् ।
तस्याहं निग्रहं मन्ये वायोरिव सुदुष्करम् ॥६-३४॥

chanchalam hi manah krishna pramaathi balavad-dridham
tasyaaham nigraham manye vaayoriva sudushkaram

For the mind is truly fickle, O Krishna, it is impetuous, strong-willed, obstinate. I think that it is as difficult to control as the wind. (6-34)

What does the word 'yoga' REALLY mean?

If you've been paying attention, you would have noticed that the title of every chapter – in the original Sanskrit – has the word 'yoga' in it. If, like most other people, you thought yoga just meant that set of weird body-bends that your mum seems to enjoy doing so much, you're so wrong. Here's the real lowdown on the Y word.

Literally, yoga means 'to yoke together', like yoking together a couple of oxen or horses to a cart or a carriage. But in the ancient Indian texts, it is used to mean the yoking together – the bringing together – of the mind and the body. Unlike modern medicine, ancient Indian texts on medicine have always believed that disease – any disease – is a result not just of trouble and imbalances within the body but also of trouble and imbalances within the mind (anxiety, grief, anger) and the spirit (depression, hopelessness, frustration) and that the three influence one another greatly. Yoga, therefore, is not just a physical practice (weird body-bends) but also a mental and spiritual practice which yokes together body, mind and spirit and helps achieve the perfect balance between the three. This balance is supposed to be the basis of a good, happy life.

The man who compiled all the information about different kinds of yoga and put it all down, in a concise, categorized manner, was a mystery man called Patanjali.

'Mystery man' because there was more than one famous Patanjali in ancient India, and no one knows for sure whether they were all the same person or different ones. The most popular and accepted view is that the Patanjali we are interested in – the one who compiled the Yoga Sutras – lived and worked around 1,600 years ago, in 400 CE, in the region that is now Uttar Pradesh.

Our Patanjali's work forms the foundation of what we know as Ashtanga Yoga or Raja Yoga, which today has a huge following not only in India but across the world. 'Ashtanga' literally translates to 'eight limbs', and the practice and mastery of all these eight limbs of yoga are believed to lead to the perfect balance that we talked about earlier.

What are these eight limbs, then?

1. **Yama** – This 'limb' tells us how we should behave with the world, and asks us to be non-violent in thought, word and deed (Ahimsa); truthful in thought and word (Satya); to not covet something someone else has, or even desire and love too deeply what we ourselves have (Asteya); to control our desires (Brahmacharya); and to not be greedy and / or hoard things for the future (Aparigraha).

2. **Niyama** – This limb tells us what disciplines we should practise, not for the world but for our own selves. It exhorts us to be clean in body – shower regularly, brush your teeth, comb your hair, change your underwear – and mind (Shaucha);

to be satisfied with what we have and take joy in what we do (Santosha); to create a good routine and stick to it – early to bed, early to rise, recite your 12-19 times tables every morning, get out and play something for an hour every evening (Tapas); to read good writings (at the time the Yoga Sutras were written, this meant the Vedas; now it could mean any good, thought-provoking book) that provide knowledge and wisdom (Svadhyaya); and to never forget to give thanks to God and the Universe (Ishvarapranidhana).

3. **Asana** – This is what most people normally associate with the word 'yoga' – the various postures that you practise during a yoga class. Essentially, though, this limb of yoga simply urges you to keep your body in fine fettle through regular physical exercise.

4. **Pranayama** – Ever notice how often the breath is used to describe emotions? – 'He breathed a sigh of relief'; 'She gasped with fear'; 'Her face was pale with anxiety, her breathing shallow'; 'The sight was breathtaking'; 'He held his breath – what was going to happen now?' When we are calm, we breathe slow and deep; when we are stressed or angry or frightened, we breathe fast and shallow. Ashtanga Yoga believes that Pranayama, or breath control, is the first step to controlling our emotions. Makes sense, what?

5. **Pratyahara** – This practice teaches you to control your senses, by withdrawing them into yourself. It is the senses that distract you constantly – the smell of good food, the theme song of your favourite TV show, the sight of your Xbox – so controlling the senses is key.
6. **Dharana** – Now we're getting to the serious stuff. Dharana is about training the mind to focus intently on one specific object. Once you get good at this, you can proceed to . . .
7. **Dhyana** – or meditation, during which you focus intently, for longer and longer periods of time, on the same object. All your thoughts are now around and about that object. Mind control is almost at hand, and will be perfected during the next step . . .
8. **Samadhi** – During the practice of Samadhi, your focus on the object is so complete that you *become* the object. Don't get it? Never mind. Just trying to master steps 1, 2, 3 and 4 can keep most people occupied for a dozen or so lifetimes.

THE MIND

THE FIVE SENSES

६

the yoga of wisdom and knowledge ⋯⋯◄◄◄◆►►►⋯⋯ gyana vigyana yoga

IN WHICH KRISHNA REVEALS THAT HE IS EVERYWHERE, AND THAT MEANS EVERYWHERE

Arjuna did not move. Across the sacred field of Kurukshetra, the uneasy murmurs that had been rippling through the ranks of both armies grew louder, more intense.

The questions running through the minds of the soldiers on either side were the same – What in heaven's name was happening on the chariot over which the flag of the monkey god fluttered so proud and strong? Why was the mighty Gandiva – a gift from the gods to the greatest archer in the world – not at Arjuna's shoulder, where it belonged? What conversation could be so important that it needed to be conducted moments before what threatened to be history's bloodiest war began? And when would it end?

Among the commanders on each side, however, the mood was entirely contrary. On the Pandava side, the commanders looked more than a little worried. Their champion Arjuna would never let them down, but this... this... *pathetic* creature hunched over on the floor of the chariot, his body language screaming hopelessness, was not even a shadow of the fearless, straight-backed warrior they knew and trusted. On the Kaurava side, Duryodhana and his favourite brother Dushasana were allowing themselves tiny smiles of triumph. It was too soon to start celebrating, of course – like everyone else on the battlefield, they had never known Arjuna to turn his back on a fight. But from where they stood, it certainly looked, incredibly, as if Krishna was trying – and so far, failing – to coax his friend to don arms! Maybe, just maybe, their arch nemesis had chickened out at the sight of the splendour of the Kuru army, cracked under the pressure! Like vultures sensing an imminent feast, they shuffled their feet and waited.

In the chariot, Arjuna's mind was in turmoil. He understood some of what Krishna was saying, he even agreed with him, but he had always believed that the Supreme God he had worshipped all his life was a remote, inaccessible being, who lived in a faraway heaven, someone who could only be persuaded to show Himself through severe penance. Now here was his best friend, his mother's brother's son, whom he had known so well for so many years, insisting that he was the Lord himself! How was such a thing possible?

As if he had read his mind, Krishna began to speak once more.

'Know this, Partha,' said Krishna, 'very few men strive for perfection, very few try to really understand me and my true nature – most are just happy to stumble along from day to day, following orders, doing things as they have always been done, not even trying to rise above the rut, or think differently, or wonder about things. Of this handful of people who try, only one, maybe, really knows me. Therefore, let me enlighten you, let me explain to you my true nature to erase your doubts.'

Interested in spite of himself, Arjuna sat up straighter. Krishna's face looked familiar and unfamiliar at the same time. It was suffused with a strange, unearthly glow; he looked gut-wrenchingly beautiful. His voice, when he began to speak, was so deep, so mesmerizing, that Arjuna could have sat there listening to him all day.

'I am earth and water, fire and ether,' intoned Krishna, 'and the very air that trembles around you. I am the power of your mind and the depth of your understanding; I am who you think *you* are.

'I am the beginning and the end, the genesis and the dissolution. All beings take birth in me, and to me they return after death.

'I am the essence of the waters, Kaunteya, the heady fragrance of the giving earth. I am sunshine and moonlight, and the blaze of a roaring fire. I am the seed of all life; I am the life sleeping inside every seed.

'I am the wisdom of the wise, the strength of the strong; the splendour of the splendid, the breath of your breath. I am everything that the man who is free of desire, desires.

'There is nothing higher, O Dhananjaya, there is nothing *else*. All the worlds – those that you live in, those that you see around you, and everything else in between – rest upon me like pearls on a string.'

IN WHICH HE WHO IS BEYOND CLASSIFICATION INDULGES IN A BIT OF CLASSIFYING

Arjuna gazed upon his friend, transfixed.

'Every changing mood of man, Arjuna, every aspect of his contradictory behaviour, comes from me – his radiant goodness and his darkest thoughts, his shining intelligence and his dull ignorance. From me come the three Gunas (states of being) of nature – creation (Rajas), preservation (Sattva), and destruction (Tamas); and the three Gunas of man's nature – rare moments of serenity and balance (Sattva) between passionate action (Rajas) on the one hand and dangerous lethargy (Tamas) on the other.

'Though all the three Gunas come from me, Partha, none of them *is* me. But so obsessed is the world with petty classifications – creation and destruction, light and dark, balance and imbalance, good and bad, beautiful and ugly, living and non-living – that it fails to recognize me – I who am beyond classification. So caught up is the world in watching the dance of the shadows that it is blind to the light that is making the shadows.

'It is I who create this Maya – this grand illusion, this dance of shadows, this constantly changing world around you. It isn't easy to rip the veil of Maya and see the truth beyond, except for those who abandon their selfish desires and turn to me, trusting me completely. The foolish and the evil, caught in the web of Maya, believing that they are the supreme, turn away from me, give their hearts over to the demons in their nature, and are lost to me.'

Arjuna shuddered. That sounded terribly final. He didn't ever want to be lost to Krishna. He forced himself to focus harder on Krishna's words.

'And there are men whose minds, seething with desire, do not know me but pray to other gods, devotedly. Those gods give these men, on my command, the gifts they desire – wealth, power, fame, success; thus I make the devotee's faith strong in his god, thus I reveal to him that single-minded purpose is rewarded. But such gifts are only temporary; they soon return to the gods.

'And then there are those of little understanding who would give me a name, a form, a shape – a million different ones, that change from day to day; they cannot see that I am nameless, formless, changeless. But I accept all the names, all the forms – for worship in any form, offered in faith, is dear to me.

'Even among the few who do turn to me, and no other, there are four distinct kinds – those who come in times of distress; those who seek knowledge and wisdom; those who seek the riches of a good, balanced life; and, last but not the least, that rarest of the rare – the wise sage who worships me for the pure joy of it, seeking nothing, wanting nothing. Noble are they all, all four of them. But, Kaunteya, the one dearest to me, because I am dearest to him, is the sage.'

He didn't know about the worshipping bit, but as far as taking joy in Krishna's company was concerned, Arjuna knew exactly where he stood. There really was none dearer to him than the man before him.

'I know all beings, Arjuna, those that went before, those that are now and those that are to come. But, with their minds twisted by desire and anger, their vision clouded by love and hate, no one really knows me, Parantapa.

'Only those who turn to me, who work sincerely but unselfishly, who kill the ignorance of "I" and "You" in themselves, who do not think, "I did this work (so I deserve its fruit)", "This is Mine (so I will fight You if You try to take it)", "I want this (so I will do anything to prevent You from getting it)", "You are different from Me (so I will regard You with suspicion)", "You are less than I am (so I will not treat You like I would treat myself)" – and instead, see me in everything and everything in me, only they know me, I who am the Absolute.'

Lessons from the Gita

10. Single-minded devotion to a cause – any cause – will be rewarded. Choose your cause wisely.

Look around you. Not everyone is good and virtuous and noble. Many people aren't even nice. But still they seem to flourish – they are rich, or successful, or famous, or powerful, or all four. Sometimes, in addition, they are also good-looking, or popular.

Forget the big movie stars and the beauty queens and the rock stars and the sports stars, think about people you know, at your own school. The top athlete who never loses an opportunity to pick on his overweight classmate, the prefect who favours his own friends, the teachers' pet who is always laughing at the teachers behind their backs, the class topper who will always pretend to be busy when you ask her for help with a Maths problem. And yet, and yet, for all their terrible behaviour, these are the people having the best time at school. It's easy to feel that life is somehow unfair. It's easy to grudge these people their success.

But that attitude is all wrong. Success – or at least what the world calls success – does not depend on whether you are nice or mean, but on how hard you work for your goal. Look a little closer, and you will see that the champion swimmer is a winner because of the hours of practice he puts in each day, rain or shine, while his muscles scream in agony. The girl who swept the awards at the dance competition is the girl who refused to bunk her dance classes, even though it meant missing birthday parties. Even the teachers' pet of our example, you will find, has always submitted her work on time, is unfailingly polite to teachers in front of them, and is usually well prepared for class.

In the Gita, Krishna says that he ensures that those who worship other gods, single-mindedly, also get the gifts they ask for (other gods like, for instance, The God of Success in sport or music or art or academics – who demands constant practice and sacrifice, or The God Who Helps You Become Popular – who demands that you constantly work at being nice to everyone, even when you've done really badly in your exams and all you want to do is snarl at them). Krishna says he does this to 'make the devotee's faith steady'. In other words, he does this so that the message goes out to the world, loud and clear, that hard, honest work and single-minded focus is always rewarded.

But, Krishna adds, the gifts that these gods hand out are like rolling trophies – you have to pass them on after a while. Next year, there will be a new student who thrashes the swimming champion, or a junior who is so smart and funny or has such a cool sense of style that today's Ms Popular will drop off the charts without a trace. The teachers' pet who was sneakily passing on information about her classmates as part of her single-minded devotion to The God Who Helps You Become Popular with Teachers, will sooner or later get ticked off by a teacher who does not approve of such sneakiness, or she may be shunned by her classmates.

Now, if the swimmer was only practising so hard because he wanted to be the champion, and not because he enjoyed making the effort to be the best that *he* could be, he will be devastated when he is beaten. If Ms Popular was only being nice to everyone because she wanted to be popular and not because she was genuinely a sweet person, she will go into depression when someone else takes her place. If the teachers' pet was only reporting her classmates to earn favour with her teachers, and not because she thought it was her duty to report bad behaviour like bullying, or cheating in exams, she will be very embarrassed when she is 'found out'. None of which is a happy situation.

The thing to do, therefore, is to work hard and make the sacrifices, but not to win what you know is a rolling trophy. The thing to do, knowing that the Universe will reward single-minded devotion to a cause, is to choose your cause wisely. Make sure the cause is unselfish and does not hurt anyone else. Make sure that you are not working for it because you want something out of it, or because you want to show up someone else, but simply because it is right, because it needs to be done.

And you will find that the rewards that such an effort will bring you – self-confidence, a quiet inner happiness, peace of mind – are the long-lasting, precious kind, the kind that no one can ever take away from you.

It's six of one and half a dozen of the other

We humans like nothing better than to classify things and people, put them in neat tiny boxes and find reasons for why two people are the same or why they are different. We like to divide people on the basis of the colour of their skin, the country they belong to, the food they eat, the amount of money they make and the gods they worship.

We do it because it makes us feel that we are in control and because we can then decide to which groups we belong. It helps us divide the world into People Like Us, whom we understand and feel comfortable with, and People Not Like Us, whom we do not understand, and therefore are not comfortable with. It is the reason there is so much hate in the world, why wars between countries begin, why people who worship one form of god are hostile to people who worship another form of god.

Which is all quite ridiculous, because, according to the Gita, God Himself – and yes, there *is* only one of Him, or Her, or It, no matter what we may think – doesn't care how we worship Him, what form we give Him in our imaginations, or by what name we call Him – Ishvar, Allah, Jesus, Wahe Guru... As long as the worshipper's heart is pure and his faith is strong, He accepts the worship happily, and gives of His blessings generously.

Here, in the original Sanskrit, is the shloka in which Krishna tells Arjuna this supreme truth, for you to enjoy.

यो यो यां यां तनुं भक्तः श्रद्धयार्चितुमिच्छति ।
तस्य तस्याचलां श्रद्धां तामेव विदधाम्यहम् ॥७-२१॥

Yo yo yaam yaam tanum bhaktah shraddhayaar-
chitum-ichchhati
Tasya tasyaachalaam shraddhaam taameva
vidadhaamyaham

In whatever form any devotee with faith wishes to worship, I make his faith unwavering. (7-21)

8

the yoga of the imperishable absolute ---◄◄◄◆▶▶▶---
aksharabrahma yoga

IN WHICH KRISHNA REVEALS HIS ADDRESS AND PROVIDES A ROADMAP FOR GETTING THERE

'Stop, stop, stop, Krishna,' Arjuna looked up at Krishna, a glazed look in his eyes. 'You say you are the Absolute, but what does Absolute really mean? You say I should "kill the ignorance of 'I' in myself", but if I am not I, who *am* I? You say I am foolish to think that I am the doer of my actions, but if I am not the doer, who is? You? Do you think you could explain all this in a little more detail, Purushottama?'

Krishna smiled. 'I will try, Arjuna, but the answers are not easy to understand, because you have never thought of the world this way.' There was a pause as Krishna gathered his thoughts. 'Think of the Absolute as light, if you will, Arjuna – formless, invisible, untouchable, indestructible, but very much there, around you and in you. When there is light, the world comes into being; when there is no light, the world disappears. It's the same with me. If it wasn't for me, there would be nothing – not you, not the world, not anything.'

Arjuna still looked doubtful.

'You think you are the doer of your actions, Partha. You think, for instance, that *you* are seeing the world. But if there was no light, would you be able to see it? Without light, without me, there would not even be a world to see! But people forget that they exist only because of me; they imagine that they exist, and function, and live their lives in a certain way, purely because of their own actions. This is what I call the ignorance of the "I".'

Around the chariot flying the Hanuman flag, horses whinnied nervously, echoing the mood of their riders. Armour clanked as soldiers flexed their sword arms and hefted their bows onto their shoulders, frustrated by the inexplicable delay.

A chill ran down Arjuna's spine. So lost had he been in Krishna's words that he had forgotten where he was,

but suddenly he could smell death in the air, poised and ready, at the edges of the battlefield.

He turned to his friend and asked him the question that had appeared unbidden in his head.

'When it is time to go, Krishna, time for a man to leave the world, how can he make sure that his soul comes to you and to no other?'

'Simply by making sure that he is thinking of me at the time of his departure,' said Krishna. 'If he does that, he will come to me, of that there is no doubt. For you see, Partha, the soul goes to that which the mind has been thinking about in its last moments. If a man has been thinking of worldly things, into the world will his soul be reborn. But if a man has his mind focused on me, straight to me will he come, never to return to its worldly existence.'

'But how can one make sure that he is thinking of you at the moment of his departure?' asked Arjuna anxiously. 'None of us knows when that time will come!'

Krishna smiled. 'That's why I say to you, Kaunteya, at all times, remember me. Meditate on me, the all-seeing, the all-knowing, the radiant sun beyond the darkness. Shut off your senses, still your thoughts, and focus on me and me alone at all times.

'Don't look so worried, Partha. For the man who has been conscious of me his entire life – worshipping me, delighting in me, reflecting on me in every waking moment, offering his every action up to me as a sacrifice – thinking of me at the time of departure is not difficult. After all, he thinks of me all the time, and his ability to meditate on me, even in the midst of his other duties, has been perfected by long and disciplined practice.'

Arjuna nodded. It was nothing but rigorous and regular practice that had made him master of the bow that now lay, inert, at his feet.

'Nothing in the Universe, Arjuna, escapes the constant cycle of birth and death. Just like the earth, the Universe also has a day and a night, each lasting a thousand ages. At the dawn of each long day, all that was asleep comes alive in the light. Night falls, and everything dissolves once again into the stillness of the dark. They have no choice.

'But beyond the constantly changing Universe, beyond everything that takes birth, lives and dies, over and over again, is something that is never born and never dies, which is constant and unchanging. That is the Absolute, Partha; that is where I live.

'And *that* is where the man who meditates on me in his last moments goes when he leaves his body. Never again will this yogi need to return to the sufferings of human life. He is never reborn, O Best of the Bharatas, he is forever free.'

Echoes of the Gita

In the Gita, Krishna asks Arjuna to stop thinking of himself as the doer of his actions. Like everyone else on earth, Arjuna is only here to play his part in a production that has been running for a long, long time. Krishna did nothing but launch the production, but that one action of his led to various reactions, each of which became the starting point of other actions and their respective reactions, and so on and on, until it reached the point where Arjuna entered the scene.

And that's why, says Krishna, it is silly of Arjuna to get attached to his actions, or their results. After all, Arjuna's 'script' – the part he has to play in the production – is a result of how the story has built up over all these years. His actions are really the result of a million other actions of a million other people since the production began. Similarly, the *results* of his action are dependent on so many other actions by so many other people. In other words, Arjuna has absolutely no control over them. All Arjuna can do, should do, says Krishna, is to focus on playing his part to the best of his ability.

William Shakespeare, the English playwright and poet, apparently agreed with Krishna that we have little control over the script of our lives. Here's an excerpt from a famous passage in his play, *As You Like It*:

The Seven Ages of Man

All the world's a stage,
And all the men and women merely players:
They have their exits and their entrances;
And one man in his time plays many parts,
His acts being seven ages. At first, the infant,
Mewling and puking in the nurse's arms.
Then the whining schoolboy, with his satchel
And shining morning face, creeping like snail
Unwillingly to school. And then the lover,
Sighing like furnace, with a woeful ballad
Made to his mistress' eyebrow. Then a soldier,
Full of strange oaths and bearded like the pard,
Jealous in honour, sudden and quick in quarrel,
Seeking the bubble reputation
Even in the cannon's mouth. And then the justice,
In fair round belly with good capon lined,
With eyes severe and beard of formal cut,
Full of wise saws and modern instances;
And so he plays his part. The sixth age shifts
Into the lean and slippered pantaloon,
With spectacles on nose and pouch on side;
His youthful hose, well saved, a world too wide
For his shrunk shank; and his big manly voice,
Turning again toward childish treble, pipes
And whistles in his sound. Last scene of all,
That ends this strange eventful history,
Is second childishness and mere oblivion,
Sans teeth, sans eyes, sans taste, sans everything.

Roopa Pai

The vanara *who rode shotgun*

In a truly epic mash-up, Hanuman, one of the most beloved characters of India's other blockbuster bestseller, the Ramayana, ends up riding into war with our hero, Arjuna, in the Mahabharata, transfigured into an icon on the flag atop his chariot. Considering that the events of the Ramayana are supposed to have happened in an entirely different era from those of the Mahabharata, how could this be possible? And, more importantly, why did Hanuman do it?

Once, so the story goes, Arjuna was on a pilgrimage. By and by, he arrived at the coastal town of Rameswaram (in present-day Tamil Nadu). As he walked along the seaside, someone pointed out to Arjuna the remnants of the bridge that Rama's *vanara* army had helped him build to cross the sea to Ravana's capital, Lanka, where Rama's beloved, Sita, was a prisoner. Arjuna wondered aloud why someone as proficient at archery as Rama would have needed the help of monkeys to build a bridge when he could have simply built it himself, with arrows.

At this, a little monkey who had been following Arjuna leaped up on to rock in front of him, chuckling heartily. 'O great hero,' he said, 'you would not ask such a foolish question if you knew just how strong and mighty the monkey heroes of old were. Sugreeva, Nala, Neela, Angada, Hanuman – no bridge of arrows could have supported them. Why, I bet no bridge of arrows could even support *my* weight!'

Arjuna, being Arjuna, was stung to the quick. 'Let's put this to the test, shall we, monkey?' he growled, shooting off several quiverfuls of arrows to construct a bridge.

The little monkey jumped on to the bridge to stress-test it. It had hardly walked 10 steps before the bridge collapsed.

'I'd like to try again,' said Arjuna. 'If I fail this time, I shall throw myself into the fire.' Sending up a silent prayer, he shot his arrows closer together, and built a bridge that was strong and true. But once again, the bridge collapsed when the monkey walked on it.

Thoroughly shamed, Arjuna built a fire and was about to throw himself into it when a young chap walking by asked him exactly what he thought he was up to. Arjuna explained.

'Did you have a referee for your contest, though?' asked the young fellow.

Arjuna shook his head.

'Well then, the bet is off! Why don't you try one last time? I volunteer to be referee.'

For the third time, Arjuna built a bridge. This time – surprise, surprise! – the bridge did not collapse under the monkey's weight, no matter what the monkey did. Exasperated, Hanuman, for it was he who was the monkey, took on his mighty form – the form he had used to leap the ocean – but the bridge still held miraculously.

Arjuna, who had already figured out who the monkey was, now realized with a start that the 'referee' was none other than Lord Vishnu himself, and that the reason the bridge still stood was not because Arjuna had suddenly got more skilful at building bridges, but because the Lord had made it so. The same realization hit Hanuman. Both of them fell at the young man's feet and begged forgiveness for their arrogance.

Then Hanuman turned to Arjuna. 'May I show how sorry I am for my behaviour by protecting your chariot in the Great War that is coming?' he said.

Arjuna bowed. 'It would be my honour and my privilege to have you on my side, Mighty Hanuman.' And that's how Hanuman got to be part of the war at Kurukshetra.

Oh, and the puzzling bit about Hanuman still being around so many years later? Well, according to Hindu mythology, Hanuman is one of the Immortals, the Chiranjeevis. Now you know.

Lessons from the Gita

11. Multi-thinking is a vital skill for a happy life. All you need is practice, practice, practice.

You've heard of multitasking – the art of doing many things at the same time with equal focus. Women are supposed to be brilliant at it, men the exact opposite. Whether that's true or not, what is true is that young people are absolute rock stars at it. They are able to listen to music, text a friend on the phone, carry on a conversation with another on Skype, and message someone else on Facebook, all while watching TV.

Multi-thinking – you heard the word here first – is similar, except that this one's the art of having more than one stream of thought running in your head constantly. It is something Krishna brings up in this chapter when he tells Arjuna that an easy way for a man to become one with God after his death is to think of Him all the time, throughout his life, no matter what activity or other thinking he is doing. In other words, Krishna recommends that thoughts of God should run as a parallel stream to every other thought flowing through a man's head, all the time.

But is such a thing really possible? Can you keep thinking about something that is completely unrelated to what you are doing at a particular time? Of course! Let's say tomorrow is the last day of your final exams and that your summer vacations begin immediately after. Notice how, even while you are in the throes of studying for your last exam, there is a parallel happy thought-track running on a loop in your head, which is all about the movie you're going to watch with your friends right after the exams and the sleepover you're going to after that?

Not all parallel thought-tracks are as easy to keep running in your head as this one, though. And it is your ability to keep the *difficult* ones running that will actually help you live a happier life.

If your main thought-track when you are, say, playing a match, goes: 'I *have* to loft that bowler for a six; I *have* to smash that forehand winner; I *have* to head that ball into goal; I *have* to win!', your parallel thought-track could go: 'I just have to play my best game every minute, because if I do, I know it won't matter whether I win or lose'.

If your main thought-track when you are doing your homework goes: 'I *hate* biology; Ms X is such a *tyrant* — she gives us such tough math worksheets; What's the *point* of studying stupid history dates, anyway?', your parallel thought-track could be: 'I know everything I'm doing today is helping me become smarter in some way, and that's always a good thing.' The positive, calming parallel tracks will balance the negative, aggressive main tracks, making you feel better after the game or through the homework process.

If your main thought-track when you're doing an annoying chore for your mum goes: 'How come she always picks a weekend for this when she knows I might have other plans?'; 'How come she always picks on me and lets my brother get away scot-free?'; 'Why can't she just do it herself?', your parallel thought-track could go: 'Since I have to do it anyway, I might as well get it over with quickly and cheerfully instead of ruining my mood for the rest of the day'; or 'I know she picks me for this because she trusts me to do it well, so I should'; or 'It is a small thing to do for her in return for all that she does for me'; or even, 'Oh, stop snivelling and get on with it – it only takes an hour!'

According to the Gita – and Krishna says this many, many times in many, many ways – it is only through regular and rigorous practice that anything is mastered. But you knew that already. Music, dance, karate, golf, maths, cooking, seeing the bright side of things, whatever it is you want to master, there is no better route – and sometimes no *other* route – than to do it over and over again until it becomes muscle memory, until you can do it without even thinking about it.

Practice works brilliantly in the case of parallel thought-tracks too. If you are good about switching on your parallel thought-tracks *every* time you are in match-mode or homework-mode or chore-mode, they will eventually begin to switch *themselves* on. In fact, if you are really, *really* disciplined about this, your parallel thought-track could one day become your main thought-track! When that happens, it's out with the negative thoughts and in with the positive, out with the anger and selfishness and in with the calm and contentment, forever. Sounds like a good thing to work towards, what?

Remember to remember

तस्मात्सर्वेषु कालेषु मामनुस्मर युध्य च ।
मय्यर्पितमनोबुद्धिर्मामेवैष्यस्यसंशयः ॥८-७॥

Tasmaat-sarveshu kaaleshu maamanusmara
yudhya cha
Mayy-arpita-manobuddhir-maamey-vaishyasya-
asanshayaha

Therefore, Arjuna, at all times, think of me and fight.*
With your mind and intelligence fixed on me, you will
attain me without doubt.

Yes, apparently, that's all it takes. Whatever you do, remember to remember the divine. In other words,

---

*Here, Krishna doesn't mean only the Kurukshetra war, but the war that Arjuna, and all of us, fight each day against the forces of greed and desire and jealousy and anger and selfishness that rage inside us.

remember, each day, to thank the Universe for the gifts it so generously showers, remember to step back and see the big picture, remember to count your blessings.

Of the hundreds of thousands gathered on the battlefield, and the hundreds and thousands waiting at home, only two were completely immune to the restless energy around them. One was Krishna himself, and the other was the royal charioteer, Sanjaya, who with his all-seeing eyes knew exactly how this would end for the Kauravas. Only out of compassion for his blind king did Sanjaya sit as patiently as he did beside Dhritarashtra, narrating to him the events at Kurukshetra as they unfolded.

'And the Blessed Lord said to Arjuna,' said Sanjaya, "To you, O Faultless One, to you who are full of unquestioning faith in me, I shall reveal now the emperor of all secrets. It requires no effort to understand, it is effortless to practise, and the one who follows it will be liberated from sorrow. Walk this path, and you will escape forever from the endless cycle of birth and death, and come to me forever."'

Dhritarashtra could not believe his ears. Capricious fate had always been kind to him, consistently handing him undeserved privileges on a platter. Kingship should never have been his, given his terrible handicap, but Pandu had inexplicably walked away from it, and it had fallen into his lap like a ripe, juicy fruit. His sons should never have been kings themselves, or at least not of the entire kingdom. But Pandu's sons had come to a game of dice that they suspected was rigged - simply because it was not right for a Kshatriya to refuse a challenge - and lost their half of the kingdom to his boys. And now, for no reason that he could fathom, he, instead of all the other, far more worthy, men on the battlefield, was going to be privy to what Krishna promised was the greatest secret in the world.

Dhritarashtra leaned forward eagerly in his seat.

९

the yoga of sovereign knowledge and sovereign mystery ········◄◄◄◆▶▶▶······· rajavidya rajaguhya yoga

IN WHICH KRISHNA LETS ARJUNA IN ON THE GREAT SECRET

Somewhere in his gut, Arjuna also realized that what was coming next was going to be tremendous, life-altering. With his heart full of faith and his ears straining to catch every last syllable that Krishna spoke, Arjuna waited.

'Once again I say to you, Parantapa, Scorcher of Foes, understand my true nature, who or what I really am. Everything you see and do not see in the Universe comes from me, lives in me, is supported by me, but none of them *is* me. Behold my divine mystery, Partha – I contain entire universes, but entire universes cannot contain me.'

'Think of me as infinite space, the space around and above and below you – the grand theatre of the suns and the stars and the mighty wind; which holds the seed of everything in the Universe; from which worlds emerge and into which they eventually dissolve.

'Just like space, which itself remains unaffected and unchanged by all the activity in it and around it, so am I completely unmoved and unchanged by the activities of the beings in me. I am just the backdrop, Kaunteya, the impartial observer of everything that goes on. I do not favour one being over another; they are all the same to me – just like space, without which neither the biggest stars nor the tiniest atoms* would exist – for what would they exist *in* then, what would they exist *on*? – am I. Without me to hold them, no being, or non-being, could exist.

'It is because of Nature – Prakriti – not because of me, that the world revolves and the sun rises and the tides recede with the setting of the moon. It is Nature that gives birth to things moving and unmoving, and it is according to its laws that everything that is born eventually dies. I, Partha, am the Master of Nature, the one who sets it in motion. It is under my supervision that the whole drama unfolds. But understand this – I myself am above Nature, outside of Nature; Nature could not exist without me, but I have always existed, with or without Nature.

'People do not understand this, Kaunteya – they do not understand that everything, everyone, flows from me, and that I am in all of them. People despise me when I am clad in a human body – they treat their fellow humans badly, not recognizing me in them.

---

*If you have studied the structure of atoms in your Science class, you know that everything in the Universe is made up of atoms and that ninety-nine per cent of every atom is empty space.

'There are people who worship gods who have forms and names, with great faith. They perform all the rituals recommended in the holy books, they can recite the Vedas* in their sleep. They offer sacrifices to their gods, hoping for a good life in heaven after their deaths. And their sacrifices are rewarded, make no mistake about that – they enjoy the fruits of their good deeds for a while in heaven, but once their rewards are exhausted, they return to earth once again – such men do not escape the cycle of birth and death.

'But those who understand my true nature, who see me in everything and everything in me; who understand that all the

---

*The oldest scriptures of Hinduism, considered to be revelations.

different forms in which I am worshipped, and all the different names people call me, are just versions of the Supreme Me, that none of those gods is me and that all of those gods are me; who meditate on me devotedly at all times, unwavering in their faith; those men and women, whether they are soldiers or merchants or scholars or farmers, whether they know the entire text of the Vedas or know not a word, whether they are considered saints or sinners; whether they offer me great riches or a handful of water – I will take care of them; I will give them what they need and protect what they have.

'This is the secret, Kaunteya – no action is good or evil if it is done as an offering to me, with complete devotion. And so I say to you, whatever you do, whatever you eat, whatever you offer, whatever you give away, all your prayers, all your rituals – do them as an offering to me. Fix your mind on me, worship me, revere me, be devoted to me, make me your goal, Partha, and to me you shall come when your days are done, never to return.'

Lessons from the Gita

12. (a) No action is itself good or evil. It is intent that makes it so. (b) Actions – all actions – have consequences.

In this chapter, Krishna says that saints and sinners are all the same to him. The Gita actually has him saying, 'Even if a man of the most vile conduct worships me with undistracted devotion, he must be reckoned as righteous.' He also says that no action is good or evil as long as it is done as an offering to him. If that is true, what is the point of being good and doing right action? Far easier to do what we like, as long as we offer the action to God and remember to say our prayers after, right? But that, apparently, is not how it works.

You see, Hinduism believes very seriously in the process of cause and effect. Your smallest action (the cause), sets off a chain of reactions (the effect), which you cannot control, let alone imagine. 'Right' actions – actions that are unselfish, responsible, and not performed out of anger or greed – usually lead to good consequences, 'wrong' actions usually lead to bad ones.

But here's the tricky part – there are no guarantees! Even right actions can sometimes lead to the wrong consequences, because of someone *else's* right or wrong action – after all, you don't function alone in the world. Let's say your uncle speeds through a red light at a four-way traffic signal because you are late for a movie.

Another car coming in from the road on the left, whose signal is actually green, is forced to brake suddenly to avoid your car. A bike that is just behind this car slams into it, and the biker's wife, who is riding pillion with a little baby, falls off and gets badly hurt. At the same time that the lady and her baby are getting admitted into hospital, you are lining up to buy popcorn. Your wrong action has led to – at least as far as you know – right consequences (you made it on time for the movie, and no policeman caught you); you have no idea about the wrong consequences that your action has caused. The other car's right action – braking to avoid hitting your car even though its driver had the right to go through – has led to terrible consequences for the third person. You see how this works?

Very often, it looks to us as if the sinners are getting away scot-free and the saints are suffering, but the reality is far more complex than we realize, simply because it is impossible for us to see the whole picture. We certainly cannot change the seemingly random – and seemingly unfair – things that happen to good people and bad people around us. The one thing we can do, however, is to add our bit to the fund of right actions in the world by doing right actions ourselves. It is all a matter of balance, really, and common sense – the more people do right actions, the more the balance of the world will tip towards rightness, and we will all have a better world to live in.

What about the Gita's statement that no action is good or evil by itself? Most of us would agree that killing another person is *bad*, EVIL. But what if that person was hurting someone else, and would have killed them if someone hadn't killed him? According to the Gita, it is all about the intent behind the action, not the action itself. If the action is unselfish (i.e., you are getting nothing out of it, not even pleasure), if the action is not driven by anger or greed or desire, if the action is something you believe is your duty to do (a soldier's duty is to fight – and kill – the soldiers of the other side, a hangman's duty is to hang convicted criminals), it is right action, whatever the action is.

Remember, though, that even though you may do the action in the exact spirit that the Gita recommends, you may still have to face consequences. Suppose X, like Dexter in the TV series, decides that Y needs to be killed, because he is a terrible person, and goes ahead and murders him. If X is caught, Man's laws, society's laws, will ensure that X is put away for life at the very least. But God's law, says the Gita, will ensure that X will enjoy great inner peace.

And then the Gita goes one step further. Even if we slip into the worst kind of wrong action, it says, even if Man's law hands us the worst punishment there is, there's no need to despair. If we are truly sorry about what we have done, if we sincerely try to reform, God's law will treat us just the same as a saint, and we will be rewarded with as much inner peace and happiness as anyone else.

That's a nice warm blanket of a thought to snuggle into at night, don't you agree?

All He needs is love

पत्रं पुष्पं फलं तोयं यो मे भक्त्या प्रयच्छति ।
तदहं भक्त्युपहृतमश्नामि प्रयतात्मनः ॥९-२६॥

Patram pushpam phalam toyam yo mey bhaktyaa prayachchhati
Tadaham bhaktyu-pahrtam-ashnaami prayataatmanaha

If one offers me a leaf, a flower, a fruit, or a little water, with devotion and a heart that is pure, I will accept that gift of love. (9-26)

If you think about it, all the things that the Gita mentions in this verse as valid offerings to God – leaves, flowers, fruits and water – are freely and generously available in Nature, even to the poorest of the poor. In one stroke, through this single, deceptively simple verse, the Gita makes it clear that God does not belong to the privileged. He does not need gold and fine silks and sumptuous food.

All He needs is love.

१०

the yoga of manifestation ⸺⸺ vibhuti yoga

IN WHICH ARJUNA DEMANDS – AND GETS – A VERY LONG LIST

'And once again, Mahabahu, hear my supreme word. I declare it to you, dearest one, and to no other, because you take such delight in listening.'

Arjuna sat before Krishna, transfixed, gazing up at this familiar-unfamiliar being who stood before him, speaking words of such beauty, such reassurance and such love. Kurukshetra, the bloody war about to begin, friends, brothers, the morning chill – everything was forgotten as Arjuna gazed at Krishna, his mind, his intelligence, all his senses, his entire being, focused on his friend's radiant face and his words.

'No one, Partha – not the greatest sages,' said Krishna, 'not the wise scholars, not even the gods – know my origins, for I was before any of them ever were. From me they all came forth, just like everything else – patience, truth, self-control, understanding, knowledge, contentment, pleasure and pain, fear and fearlessness, fame and infamy, existence and non-existence, everything you see and feel and know, and its opposite. I am the origin of all, from me does everything proceed.

'The wise know this and worship me with no doubt in their hearts, no distraction in their devotion. With their thoughts in me, their very lives in me, they constantly tell the world about me – for they have no other conversation – and they are joyous and content. And in them, because I love them so, I destroy the darkness of ignorance with the shining lamp of wisdom.'

At these words, a thrill of joy and recognition shot through Arjuna like a bolt of lightning. This was the Lord Incarnate who stood before him, and none other! He would not have been able to explain why he now knew it with such certainty, but know it he did. He fell to his knees and clasped his hands, his eyes brimming with tears of love and gratitude.

'I believe, I believe, Keshava!'

The floodgates opened. Words of adoration burst from Arjuna and would not be stanched.

'O Param Brahma! Param Dhama! O Eternal, Divine Being, Lord of all Creatures, He who is never born, He who is everywhere! O Purushottama, best among men, Lord of the World, God of gods, I believe You; how could I not, when I hear from your own lips what the sages have always said about You?

'Tell me, tell me *now*, O Yogi beyond compare, because no one but You can do it, how will I know You? Though I understand now that You are the Absolute, without name, without form, I am a mere mortal of little understanding and it is too difficult for me to think of You that way. I want names, I want forms! Tell me, Blessed Lord, exactly what to think about when I want to think about You. Give me the entire list, don't leave anything out, for your words are like honey to my ears, Janardhana, and I don't want You to ever stop speaking.'

Krishna smiled. 'As you wish, Gudakesha.

'Of the twelve great sons of Aditi, mother of the gods, I am the foremost, Vishnu; of all the lights, I am the glorious sun; of all the stars that twinkle in the night sky, I am the radiant moon. Of the four Vedas, I am the lyrical Samaveda; of all the gods in heaven, I am the king, Indra; of all the senses, I am the mind, who controls them.

'Of the eleven Rudras that sprang from Shiva, I am the origin, Shiva; of the eight Vasus, the gods of the elements, I am fire, Agni; of the Yakshas and the Rakshasas, who hoard great riches underground, I am their lord, Kubera; and of all the mountain peaks, I am the greatest, Meru.

'Of the priests, I am the guru of the gods, Brihaspati; of the great sages I am the venerable Bhrigu; among immovable things, I am the mighty Himalaya; of all the

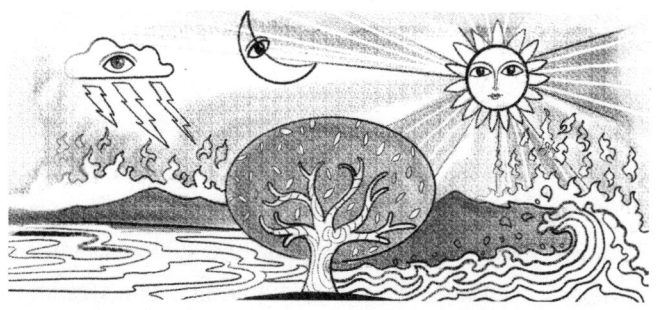

words that are spoken, I am the divine syllable Om. Of all trees, I am the sacred peepul, Ashvattha; of horses, I am Uchchaishravas, the seven-headed flying horse; of the elephants, I am the four-tusked Airavata.

'Of weapons, I am Vajra, the thunderbolt, which never misses its mark; of the cows, I am Kamadhenu, the miraculous wish-giving cow; of the serpents, I am Vasuki, who offered himself as the rope during the Churning of the Ocean; of the Nagas, the snake people, I am Ananta, who is coiled around the Universe. Of the water-dwellers, I am Varuna, lord of the oceans; of those who uphold the law, I am the god of righteousness, Yama; of all things that cleanse and purify, I am Vayu, the wind god.

'Of all the beasts, I am the lordly lion; of all the birds, I am the mighty man-bird Garuda; of all warriors, I am the peerless Rama; of all the rivers, I am the sacred Ganga. Of all the months, I am the pleasant Margashirsha; of all the seasons, I am the flower-bearing spring; of all those who create and bring forth new life, I am the god of love, Kama, who ensures it happens at all.

'Of all the members of the ancient clan of the Vrishnis, I am the foremost, Vasudeva; of all the sacred chants, I am the powerful Gayatri mantra; of all the letters, I am the first, A; of all the Pandavas, I am noble Arjuna.

'I am the beginning, the middle and the end of all beings; I am the origin of all existence, and I am all-devouring death, which is the origin of things to come. I am the silence in the secret and the splendour in the splendid, I am imperishable Time and certain victory. I am the seed of all existence, Arjuna, nothing can be that doesn't start and end with Me.

'What more can I say to you, Parantapa, but that this list goes on and on, endlessly, and that what I have revealed thus far is only a tiny glimpse into my infinite glory. That anything that you see around you that is glorious and graceful and mighty has sprung from a mere spark of my splendour. What more do you need to know, Partha, than that the entire Universe is supported on an infinitesimal fraction of Me?'

When you see it, you will know

यद्यद्विभूतिमत्सत्त्वं श्रीमदूर्जितमेव वा ।
तत्तदेवावगच्छ त्वं मम तेजोंऽशसम्भवम् ॥१०-४१॥

Yad yad vibhootimat-sattvam shreemad-oorjitam-eva vaa |
tatta-devaa-vagachchha tvam mama tejonsha-sambhavam

Whatever is glorious and majestic and full of vigour and energy, know that it has sprung from a fragment of my splendour. (10-41)

It's simple, says the Gita. Anything that you see or hear around you that makes you catch your breath in awe and wonder at its beauty and energy – a piece of music, a work of art, a fabulously designed building, a tree in bloom, moonlight on a still lake, an athlete in her prime, an unusually gifted child – springs from a power greater than all of us, and is proof that it exists.

Fantastic beasts and where to find them

Hindu mythology is bursting at the seams with fabulous beasts and birds that are extraordinary versions of beasts and birds on earth. Unlike in western mythology, where many such fantastic creatures are considered 'evil', or at least a nuisance – dragons, for example, imprison princesses in towers, breathe fire and have to be destroyed by the hero of the story – there are no inherently 'evil' creatures in Hindu mythology.

Here's a quick 101 on four fantastic beasts that Krishna mentions in this chapter of the Gita.

Airavata – Also called the 'elephant of the clouds', this white, four-tusked elephant stands guard at the gates of Devaloka, abode of the Hindu gods. Different versions of Airavata show him with three, five or seven heads, but all versions agree that he is the vehicle of Indra – god of rain and thunder, and king of Devaloka. The really fascinating story about Airavata is this, though – once, a demon called Vritra captured all the waters of the earth, refusing to let them flow. There was no rain, and the earth became dry and barren. As protector of the earth and its people, Indra came after Vritra on Airavata. While the battle raged, Airavata reached into the underworld with his mighty trunks, sucked the water out of underground reservoirs and sprayed the clouds with it. The rain came down in torrents and was lapped up gratefully by the parched earth. Of course, Indra won in the end, but the more interesting part of this story is Airavata's role. So much more fun to learn about how the water cycle works through this story than the way Science textbooks teach it, don't you think?

Uchchaishravas – One of the best-known stories in Hindu mythology is the one about the Churning of the Ocean of Milk. Mount Meru (which Krishna calls the greatest of mountains in this chapter) was used as the churn, while Vasuki the serpent offered himself as the rope. With the gods holding one side of the 'rope' and the demons the other, the ocean was churned to bring up Amrit, the nectar of immortality, which lay deep inside. Before the pot of Amrit came up, however, several other treasures were churned up, including the snow-white, seven-headed flying horse, Uchchaishravas, who became the vehicle of Mahabali, king of the demons. Once, when Uchchaishravas was flying across the sky, Vinata and Kadru, two sisters watching him from the earth, could not agree on whether his tail was black or white. They decided to bet on it, with the stake being that the loser would become the winner's slave for life. Kadru, who had bet that the tail was black, realized that she had been wrong – Uchchaishravas's tail was as white as the rest of him – so she asked her sons, the black snakes, to wind themselves over the horse's tail when she brought Vinata there. Vinata was fooled, and became the snakes' slave – until her own son, Garuda (see the next entry) bought her freedom back for her.

Garuda – The mighty man-bird whose wingspan is so large it covers the sun, noble Garuda is the vehicle of Lord Vishnu and the sworn enemy of serpents. His legendary strength and bravery are celebrated in every story about him, but his greatest virtue is his unselfishness. The story goes that Garuda's mother had become a slave to her nephews, the serpents, when she lost a silly bet  with her sister. To free his mother from her bond, Garuda agreed to bring the snakes Amrit, the nectar of immortality, from the gods. To get to the pot of nectar, Garuda had to get past a ring of fire that stretched across the sky, a fierce spinning disc with blades that could cut anyone to ribbons, and two deadly snakes, apart from a whole battalion of gods who tried to stop him from leaving heaven with it. But Garuda fought them all off and delivered the nectar to the snakes (however, because the snakes had helped their mother win the bet through deceit, they did not get to taste the Amrit in the end). Through all this, the noble bird did not think even once of keeping some of the nectar for himself. Pleased, Vishnu asked Garuda to be his mount, to which Garuda happily agreed.

Kamadhenu – This miraculous wish-granting cow, capable of producing weapons, armies of warriors and entire cities from within herself, is also believed to have come out of the Churning of the Great Ocean of

Milk. She is also called Surabhi, the sweet-smelling one (all cows were sweet-smelling to the ancient Indians, who were mainly agriculturists). Many different sages are supposed to have owned Kamadhenu, but all versions of stories about her agree that anybody who tried to harm her or the sage who owned her, came to a very bad end. In most cases, since the sage himself was forbidden to fight, it was Kamadhenu who produced weapons and armies to fend off the attackers. Kamadhenu is not worshipped in temples, but every wandering cow that Hindus feed on Indian city streets, in villages and in temples, even to this day, is considered an avatar of her – this is one of the reasons why Hindus worship cows even today.

Seasons in the (Indian) sun

You probably know that the Indian calendar is not really based on the western calendar. The Indian New Year is not 1 January, when everything is cold and asleep and dead, but somewhere between end-March and early April, at the beginning of spring, when the sun has chased away the last of the winter chill and new life is bursting out of everywhere. In other words, at a far more logical time to celebrate new beginnings than 1 January.

Because the Indian / Hindu calendar is based on the movements of the moon and the stars, the date of the

Indian New Year shifts slightly from year to year. So we cannot actually pin down the dates according to the western calendar, for each of the 12 Hindu months. We cannot say, for instance, that the first month, Chaitra, starts on 23 March every year. But we *can* associate each Indian month with particular festivals, for instance, or agricultural patterns. Here goes!

A dozen months . . .

- **Chaitra (March–April)** – Happy New Year! The first day of the month of Chaitra, and the first day of the Hindu calendar, is celebrated as Ugadi, Gudi Padwa, and Thapna in different parts of the country.
- **Vaishakha (April–May)** – In Punjab, it's time for the harvest festival of Baisakhi; in Kerala, Vishu is celebrated with lights and fireworks. Buddhists reckon the full-moon night of this month to be the birthday of Gautama Buddha himself, celebrating it as Buddha Purnima.
- **Jyeshta (May–June)** – As the Indian summer reaches its peak, the heat sends everyone scurrying indoors. That's probably why Hindus believe that the Goddess Ganga descended to earth in this month, and gather on her banks for a dip in her cooling waters as part of Ganga Dussehra.
- **Ashada (June–July)** – The Indian monsoons arrive, ending the scorching summer and sending people

dancing into the streets. But the torrential rains and flooding of rivers makes it an inconvenient, impractical month for celebrations like weddings and housewarmings. The Hindus have made it easier for everyone to refrain by labelling Ashada a mostly 'inauspicious' month.

- **Shravana (July–August)** – The monsoon recedes and cooler weather sets in. It's time for the Hindu festive season to begin, which kicks off with Krishna Janmashtami, the birthday of Krishna, right in the middle of the monsoon, and also includes the festival of sibling love, Raksha Bandhan.
- **Bhadrapada (August–September)** – On the fourth day, or Chaturthi, of Bhadrapada, the beloved elephant-headed god is brought home to great joy and festivities, particularly in Maharashtra and Karnataka, and Ganesha Chaturthi begins.
- **Ashvina (September–October)** – In the month of Ashvina, the Hindu festive season explodes, with Durga Puja in West Bengal, Navaratri in Gujarat and Dussehra/Dasara in most parts of the country.
- **Kartika (October–November)** – Winter is around the corner! The days are shorter, the nights are longer, and the time is therefore perfect for Diwali/Deepavali, the festival of lights, which coincides with the darkest night of the year – the new moon night of Kartika.

- **Margashirsha or Agrahayana (November–December)** – The month that Krishna calls the best of months in the tenth chapter of the Gita is nippy and lovely, the best time of the year in hot, tropical India. This is a good time to sit around in the sun, drinking chai and eating pakoras.
- **Pausha (December–January)** – The dark heart of winter, when northern India shivers, and south and west India enjoy some of the best weather of the year. Towards the end of Pausha, to commemorate the harvest of the winter crops, the whole country celebrates, calling the event by different names – Makara Sankranti, Pongal, Uttarayan, Lohri, Maghi and Bihu...
- **Magha (January–February)** – There is still a nip in the air. The trees shed their leaves, clearing the decks for their new coats of fresh green foliage, come the spring. It's time to celebrate the 'Great Night of Lord Shiva', Maha Shivaratri, the anniversary of the marriage of Shiva and Parvati.
- **Phalguna (February–March)** – Flower-bearing spring arrives in all its colourful, scented glory. The last day of Phalguna, which heralds the coming of warmer, longer days, is celebrated in the best way possible – by throwing buckets of coloured water at family and friends as part of the much-loved festival of Holi.

... And half a dozen seasons

The four seasons known in the west – summer, fall, winter and spring, in that order – are just not enough to contain and cover all the different and wonderful seasons we have here in India. That's why there are officially six seasons in the Indian calendar, each lasting two months, and each with its own evocative name. Here is the complete list.

- **Vasanta Ritu** – Beautiful spring, which, according to Krishna, is the foremost among seasons (Phalguna and Chaitra)
- **Grishma Ritu** – Blazing summer, ending with the summer solstice (Vaishakha and Jyeshta)
- **Varsha Ritu** – The great Indian monsoon (Ashada and Shravana)
- **Sharad Ritu** – Autumn, marked not so much by the shedding of leaves as by a cooling off of the earth, and some of the most important festivals of the year (Bhadrapada and Ashvina)
- **Hemanta Ritu** – Pre-winter, the most pleasant time of the year across India (Kartika and Margashirsha)
- **Shishira Ritu** – Deep winter, which ends with two weeks of severe dry weather during which many trees shed their leaves, creating a brief tropical 'fall' (Pausha and Magha)

११

the yoga of the vision of the cosmic form ----◄◄◄◆▶▶▶----
vishwaroopadarshana yoga

IN WHICH KRISHNA GRANTS ARJUNA'S WISH – AND SCARES HIM SILLY

Arjuna had not moved a muscle through Krishna's entire recitation. Now, looking adoringly at the Lord, he said, 'There is no more confusion in my mind, no more doubt, Supreme One. You have chased all my delusion away with the only truth there is – You, and no other, are the prime mover of the Universe. Birth is but the start of a journey from You; death, nothing but a homecoming, a return to You. The world changes constantly, nothing lasts – this is the law of Nature. Only You are not of this transient world, my Lotus-eyed Lord. You, and only You, are Imperishable, Never-changing.'

Arjuna stopped speaking. A wish had just blossomed in his heart, a hope so audacious it embarrassed him. 'You have been blessed enough,' he chided himself. 'The Lord himself has shared with you the greatest secret in the Universe. And you want *more*?' But the yearning would not be denied; it grew and grew until it filled his being, whispering, 'Tell him, Prince, tell him your heart's deepest desire. There is no law against asking!' In the end, the whisper won.

'Don't judge me, Parameshvara,' begged Arjuna, 'but grant me one last act of grace. I long to see You as You really are, not in this paltry human form that does no justice to your divine glory. Might my unworthy eyes feast upon your true form, my Lord? Will You show yourself to me?'

The Compassionate Lord smiled. 'So be it.'

Krishna stood tall. A glow suffused him, blurring the edges of his human form. The glow grew to a blazing light that spread out in all directions, blinding Arjuna. When Krishna spoke, his voice filled the earth and the sky.

'Behold then, Partha, my wondrous forms – hundreds, thousands, hundreds of thousands – in every shape and colour that you have imagined, and in those that you have not. Behold, O Prince, the Adityas and the Vasus, the Rudras and the Ashvins, every celestial being you have ever heard of, and those that you haven't, for they are all in Me. Behold in Me the Universe that you know, and those that you do not, see everything you wish to see, and everything you cannot bear to set eyes upon.'

Arjuna squinted into the light, eager, impatient. But all he could see was blazing whiteness. Fear and sorrow gripped him. He had always known it, and now it had been proved beyond doubt – he wasn't worthy, he wasn't!

But Krishna was speaking again, and his voice was full of compassion. 'Your human eye cannot see Me thus, O Bharata. I bestow upon you now the gift of divine sight.'

And then, Arjuna, the noble Pandava, prince among men, beheld a grand, terrible, never-before sight. Shaking and gasping, overcome by adoration, Arjuna beheld the Lord.

In the palace at Hastinapura, King Dhritarashtra held his breath, waiting for Sanjaya to speak, to fill his blind eyes with the vision of Krishna as the Lord Incarnate. But for the first time since he had known him, the articulate sage seemed to have been struck almost speechless. His wonderful facility for calm, precise expression had deserted him; instead, rough, inadequate words tumbled from Sanjaya's lips.

'And then, O King, the Master Yogi revealed to Partha his divine form, speaking from a million mouths, seeing from a million eyes, full of wondrous marvels his form, adorned with countless ethereal ornaments, holding up a multitude of divine weapons, resplendent, wearing celestial garlands and heavenly raiments, anointed with the perfumes of paradise, of boundless form, his heads turned in every direction, seeing everything ... O King, it is as if the light of a thousand suns had blazed forth from the sky, all at once, but a hundred times brighter, a million times more glorious.

'Seeing this, the Pandava's hair stands on end, O King. Wonderstruck, filled with amazement, he clasps his hands and bows his head, and begins to speak, incoherent with bliss.'

With his own hair standing on end, desperately hungry for more, Dhritarashtra leaned in to listen.

'Every god I have known, every story I have heard, I see it in You, my God,' cried Arjuna. 'Infinite are You, without beginning, middle or end, O Vishwaroopa, Form Universal! In your dazzling glow, I see the flaming fire and the brilliant sun; your sparkling crown and your mace and discus only barely visible in the shimmering golden haze of you. Your face is a blaze of light, the moon and the sun are your eyes, your radiance burns up the very Universe, O Anantabahu of the countless arms!

'You fill the sky and the earth, and all the space between them with your breathtaking form. Into You enter hosts of gods and sages, singing your praises, full of awe and fear. Gazing upon your boundless shape, wondrous, frightening, O Divine Colossus, with the infinite eyes, arms, feet, thighs and stomachs; with your mouths, terrible with many tusks, open wide, ready to devour all, your eyes glowing like coals . . . the worlds tremble, as my heart does. Be gracious, Lord of gods, be merciful!

'And now I see . . .' Arjuna's voice cracked with equal parts anguish and rapture. 'I see, my Lord, rushing towards your open mouths – like moths to a flame, like rivers to the ocean – the greatest heroes of our times. I see all the sons of Dhritarashtra, Grandsire Bhishma, Acharya Drona, the great warrior Karna and all the kings on both sides. They race headlong into your fearful mouths as if they cannot stop themselves, and are ground to dust between your gnashing teeth.

'Who *are* You, Devourer of Worlds? *What* are You, with your flaming mouths and scorching radiance? Tell me, tell me now, O Vishnu, that I may know You and worship You.'

'I am come as Time, destroyer of the worlds,' intoned the Formless One, 'who consumes all and spares none. Even without your action, Arjuna, even if you were never to raise arms against them, all the warriors you see arrayed before you will one day meet their death – Time will see to that.

'Therefore, I say to you, Partha, rise, pick up your bow, and gain glory for having done your duty as a warrior and a king; earn the right to rule your kingdom, and rule it well. Time has marked these warriors for death already, and I have already slain them. Your action will only determine the manner of their death, Savyasachi; you only strike the already doomed.

'Stand up! Slay Drona, Bhishma, Jayadratha, Karna and the other mighty warriors. Fight, Arjuna, have no fear. The enemy is yours to conquer.'

Trembling, Arjuna fell to the ground and prostrated himself before the Lord, his hands clasped in fear and adoration. 'O Hrishikesha,' he mumbled, his voice choked with emotion, 'I see now why the world rejoices in You, why the good and the wise take such delight in singing your glories, and why those who do not know You, flee from your terrible presence in fear.

'You are the highest, the first, O Primal One! You are the wind and the fire and the oceans, O Ancient Spirit, the sun and the moon, and the ultimate destroyer of everyone and everything. All hail to You, Infinite One, in whom the Universe rests; I salute You a thousand times, I bow to You from every side.'

A sudden memory, from what seemed like a lifetime ago, slammed into Arjuna's brain out of nowhere, and a shudder passed through his prostrate form.

'Forgive me, I beg, Aprameya,' he said, 'for all the times I spoke rashly to You, calling You Krishna, Yadava, Sakha, with such familiarity, not realizing who You really were. Countless are the times when I teased You and joked with You and argued with You, when we feasted together, or rested, or walked as friends among the crowd. I meant no malice, Lord, I was only careless; or maybe it was love that made me so bold.

'Be compassionate; overlook my transgressions, I beg You; bear with me, Adored One, as a father bears with his son, and a friend with his friend, and a lover with his beloved, for You are all that and more to me.

'And now, Lord of gods, I beg You to return to your old, familiar form, the form I know and love. I rejoice at what I have seen, I do; and I realize how privileged I am. But this form of yours fills me with dread; it bewilders me and robs me of my peace.'

For a moment, everything went quiet. His face still firmly on the ground, Arjuna felt rather than saw the blazing light dim, the wondrous vision recede. When the Lord spoke again, it was in his friend's voice.

'Here I am, Arjuna, your best friend, in the flesh.' Krishna raised the trembling Arjuna from where he lay prone on the ground and gathered him into his arms, comforting him.

Arjuna's heart was glad, but he knew something had changed irrevocably between the two of them – he would still love Krishna, of course, perhaps even more than he had before, if that were possible, but he would never now be able to forget who Krishna really was, and their friendship would never again be the same, easy, relationship-between-equals thing that it had been. The thought made Arjuna sad.

'Even the gods thrill to see this form of mine, Parantapa, and no man before you has seen it. I understand that it is not easy to behold, but do not be afraid any more, do not be bewildered.'

Arjuna nodded. The Lord's voice – familiar, beloved – had soothed him, and he was now calm and composed.

'Understand this, Parantapa. Not by knowing the Vedas, not by performing rituals, not by offering Me gifts and giving away alms does a man get to see Me in the form you just have. But he who offers all his work to Me, and looks upon Me as his only goal, who worships Me with unswerving devotion and looks on no creature with hate, he is blessed, and he will come straight to Me, O Pandava.'

Blast from the past

What does shloka no. 32 of the eleventh chapter of the Bhagavad Gita have to do with nuclear bombs? Let's see.

कालोऽस्मि लोकक्षयकृत्प्रवृद्धो लोकान्समाहर्तुमिह प्रवृत्तः ।
ऋतेऽपि त्वां न भविष्यन्ति सर्वे येऽवस्थिताः प्रत्यनीकेषु योधाः ॥११-३२॥

Kaalosmi lokakshaya-krit-pravriddho
lokaan-samaahartum-iha pravrittaha
Riteypi tvaam na bhavishyanti sarve
yevasthitaah pratyanikeshu yodhaahaa

I am come as Time, world-destroying, mature, engaged constantly in subduing the world. Even without your action, all the warriors arrayed on the opposite side shall one day cease to be. (11:32)

Rewind to the mid-20th century. The infamous Manhattan Project, a secret American research and development project to produce the world's first nuclear weapons, had been in operation since 1939, the year the Second World War began. Finally, in 1945, scientists on the project were ready with a prototype. On 7 May, the test bomb, code-named 'The Gadget' was detonated in the Jornada del Muerto desert in New Mexico, in what came to be known as the Trinity Test.

Trinity was a huge success for the team, and especially for physicist J. Robert Oppenheimer, the director of the Los Alamos Laboratory where the bomb had been developed. A few months later, a bomb just like The Gadget would be used to flatten the Japanese city of Nagasaki, eventually kill as many as 75,000 people, and effectively end the Second World War.

The destructive power of the bomb that they had developed was not something that all the scientists who had worked on it were comfortable with. In a television interview many years later (watch an excerpt here: https://www.youtube.com/watch?v=lb13ynu3Iac), Oppenheimer described his mixed feelings after the Trinity Test, in these words:

'We knew the world would not be the same. A few people laughed, a few people cried. Most people were silent. I remembered the line from the Hindu scripture,

the Bhagavad Gita; Vishnu is trying to persuade the Prince that he should do his duty, and to impress him, takes on his multi-armed form, and says, "Now I am become Death, destroyer of worlds." I suppose we all felt that, one way or another.'

(An interesting sidelight: The Sanskrit word 'Kaala' means both Time and Death. Just like death, Time favours no one, and devours everyone and everything eventually.)

Oppenheimer, who is often called 'the father of the atomic bomb', also recalled that, while watching the spectacular blast in the Mexican desert, he had remembered another shloka from the Gita (Oppenheimer knew his Gita well, obviously!). That shloka was also from this chapter – shloka no. 12.

दिवि सूर्यसहस्रस्य भवेद्युगपदुत्थिता ।
यदि भाः सदृशी सा स्याद्भासस्तस्य महात्मनः ॥११-१२॥

Divi surya-sahasrasya bhaved-yugapad-utthitaa
Yadi bhah sadrishee saa syaad-bhaasas-tasya mahaatmanaha

If the light of a thousand suns were to blaze forth all at once in the sky, that might be comparable to the splendour of the Mighty One. (11-12)

It is no surprise that it was this verse that popped into Oppenheimer's mind, for Brigadier General Thomas Farrell, one of the 10 VIPs watching the explosion, described the same sight thus: 'The lighting effects beggared description. The whole country was lighted by a searing light with the intensity many times that of the midday sun. It was golden, purple, violet, grey and blue. It lighted every peak, crevasse and ridge of the nearby mountain range with a clarity and beauty that cannot be described but must be seen to be imagined...'

Chillingly, Farrell's description is almost identical to Sanjaya's description of the wonderful, terrifying vision of Krishna in his Universal Form at Kurukshetra!

१२

the yoga of devotion ────◄◄◄◆►►►──── bhakti yoga

IN WHICH KRISHNA GIVES ARJUNA THE TRUE DEVOTION 101

Arjuna did not need any more convincing. How could he not believe – after that wondrous vision that had been granted to him – that Krishna was none other than the Lord himself? The thought of his own death had never scared him, and now, after seeing his kinsmen rushing towards their own inevitable end, without his lifting a finger, his horror at raising arms against his brothers and teachers had also receded somewhat. He understood now that death was just another step in the long, long journey of the soul towards the Absolute One. He understood now why he had no choice but to stand and fight – that was the role that had been handed to him in this lifetime, and performing that role well was not only his duty and his responsibility, but one of the easiest ways to get to the ultimate destination, to reach the Formless One.

However, Arjuna still needed to clarify a couple of things. At the moment, he had the complete attention of the Lord Incarnate, and who knew when that might happen again? For all he knew, he could be dead by sunset, and then he would never have his answers, until his next lifetime!

Arjuna decided to seize the moment. The war could wait.

'You are the Formless, Nameless One, Lord, I understand that now. But there are devotees, sincere in their devotion and their love for You, who choose to worship symbols of You – trees, cows, the sacred fire, forms that they believe to be You. They give these forms different names, call them god and friend and child and lover and mother and father. They pour their hearts into those forms, singing your praises, doing their work in your name. I am confused, Lord, and only You can clear my mind on this one. Who is the greater yogi – the one who worships You as the Absolute, or the one who chooses to worship You through a form, a name, a symbol?'

'There is no doubt, Arjuna,' said the Blessed Lord, 'that those who worship Me as the Absolute will come to Me. But it is not easy for the soul that is within a body, the soul that lives in this palace of illusions that is the world, to break free, to see the world as it really is, to see *Me* as I really am. Far easier to look for Me and find Me in my many forms that you can see and touch and hear around you, far easier to pour your love and devotion into things in which you can feel my presence. I would say that the man who can do that –

treat every man, woman and child the same, seeing Me in them; treat every creature with love, for I am in each of them; treat the earth with respect, feeling my presence in her – is the greater yogi.

'And therefore, I say to you, Partha, fix your mind and your understanding on Me alone, at every moment, whatever else you may be doing.

'If that is too difficult just now, then at least try and get there by the regular, disciplined practice of meditation, Dhananjaya. Eventually, you will be able to meditate on Me through the day, without even thinking about it.'

Arjuna looked around him, a question in his eyes, but Krishna had already sensed it.

'If your life is so full of action that it is hard to put aside time for the practice of meditation, then simply offer up your every action to Me as you do it.

'If even that is too hard, if you cannot remember to offer your actions to Me, then at least carry out your actions selflessly without any desire for reward, with no expectations of a particular result. If you can do that – just that one thing – it is enough.

'For that one thing – doing action with no desire – is far more difficult to practise than simple devotion, far harder to achieve than single-minded concentration, and brings far more peace than all the knowledge and wisdom in the world.

'Let Me say it again, clearly, simply, exhaustively; let Me define a true devotee for you, Partha:
1. He who has no ill-will towards anyone;
2. He who is friendly and compassionate;

3. He who is free of the ego, the sense of "I, Me, Mine";
4. He who is even-minded in pleasure and pain;
5. He who is always content;
6. He who has self-control and doesn't let his senses rule his mind;
7. He who has will power; whose determination is unshakeable;
8. He from whom the world does not shrink from fear or disgust or loathing;
9. He who does not shrink from the world from fear or disgust or loathing;
10. He who is free of anger and joy, fear and anxiety;
11. He whose actions do not cause grief to anyone;
12. He who does not feel grief because of anyone's actions;
13. He who has no expectations;
14. He who is pure in his thoughts;
15. He who is skilful in action;
16. He who has stopped thinking of himself as the doer of the action, and sees himself instead as part of a grand plan that involves everything else in the Universe;
17. He who is unconcerned about the results of his action;
18. He who is untroubled whatever result his action produces;
19. He who is free of desire;
20. He who does not hate;
21. He who has given up judging actions by the terms "good" and "evil";

22. He who behaves exactly the same towards friend and foe;
23. He who behaves exactly the same towards someone who has a "good reputation" and towards someone with a "bad reputation";
24. He who is free of attachment;
25. He who treats blame and praise in exactly the same way;
26. He who does not speak too much; who is restrained in his speech;
27. He who is content with whatever he has, and whatever comes his way; and
28. He who has no place he calls home; who considers the whole world to be his home and every creature in it his family.

'Such a man, Arjuna, is my devotee; such a man is dear to Me. And among such men, those who have complete faith in Me, who think of Me as their ultimate aim and rejoice in Me, they are exceedingly dear.'

Lessons from the Gita

13. You don't need to worship God to be dear to him. Just following the 'good person' rules is enough.

This is probably the most surprising of the Gita's lessons. Considering that the Gita is a religious scripture, and the holy book of the Hindus, it is astounding that it does not insist on devotion to God as one of the many requirements of a true devotee / good person / happy person / person dear to God. In this chapter, Krishna, who has just shown himself to be the Lord Incarnate, lists out a number of qualities a true devotee must have, but not one of them is about worshipping God!

Now, just for a moment, let's step back and ask ourselves an important question: What do human beings really want in life? Actually, let's tweak that a little bit. What do *you*, as a young person with your whole life ahead of you, really want in life? To be rich, to be famous, to be beautiful, to be successful? If you nodded vigorously to all of the above, take a moment to think about *why* you want to be all these things. Perhaps because you can then have a fancy car and a big house and many people to serve you and the adoration of the world and enough money to travel and eat at the best restaurants and stay in the most luxurious hotels and wear the most beautiful clothes and own the trendiest accessories? Or maybe because being rich will give you a lot of money, and being famous will give you a lot of influence, and being successful will give you a lot of power, all of which you will use to change the world, to end hunger and poverty and disease?

Great. Now think about why you *really* want those beautiful things, or why you *really* want to change the world. If you are very honest with yourself, the answer is usually, 'Because I believe that will make me happy.' Some of you probably answered this right at the beginning, in response to our first question about what you really want in life, saying, 'What I really want is to be happy.' Either way, we have established that what human beings really want, in their heart of hearts, is to be happy. The wiser ones will go a step further and say what people really want is not happiness, which is anyway a temporary state, but peace and contentment, both of which are longer-lasting, and more fulfilling.

Very few of you, if any, would have answered our first question with, 'What I really want in life is to be dear to God / to be the perfect devotee.' Which is absolutely fine. If nothing else, it is at least completely honest.

But here's the cool bit – even the Gita does not say that your answers ('I want to be rich'; 'I want to be famous'; 'I want to be happy') are bad answers, or 'wrong' answers. It does not say that 'I want to be dear to God' is the only good and right answer. In fact, in this chapter, the Gita has God Himself saying that you do not necessarily need to worship him to be dear to him, or even to get what you really want in life – peace and contentment.

Of course, a belief in God could certainly help to some extent in making you feel secure and content – it is always nice to believe that there is someone who loves you (your parents, your friends, Santa Claus...) watching out for you and planning things that will make you smile, or that the awful, unfair things that happen to you are part of some divine architect's grand plan for your life. But a belief in God, according to the Gita itself, is not *essential* to a life of peace and contentment.

What *is* essential, though, is being a good person, who wishes no one any ill will, who gives no one grief, who treats blame and praise with the same attitude, and so on, as listed so clearly by Krishna in this chapter. What is essential also, according to the Gita, is not to depend on anyone – not your parents, not your friends, not your leaders, not your heroes – for your happiness, and not to blame anyone for your unhappiness. The thing to do is to find contentment within yourself, for that is something no one can take away from you.

Just as an intellectual exercise, why don't you go through each of the points in Krishna's list and think about why *not* having that particular quality would make you unhappy, or anxious, or fearful, or angry, or jealous, or sad – any one of which would destroy your peace of mind and your sense of contentment. If you find it too difficult to do alone, do it with a group of friends, or with your family across the dinner table. You might end up being surprised at how engaging and enlightening – and fun – this could be!

१३

the yoga of the distinction between the field and the knower of the field ---◀◀◀◆▶▶▶--- kshetra kshetragya vibhaga yoga

IN WHICH KRISHNA UNRAVELS A DEEP AND COMPLEX MYSTERY

'I have yet another question for You, Keshava,' said Arjuna, the moment Krishna had finished. He was basking in the warmth of the Lord's undivided attention, and he wasn't about to let it go anytime soon. 'You have been talking about the soul as something that is separate from everything we see and hear and touch, even separate from the body itself. What is this soul, then? Where is it? How is it different and separate from everything else?'

'Think of it this way, Partha,' said the Blessed Lord. 'Think of your body as the "field of action", and your soul as the "knower of the field", who stands by quietly, watching everything that happens in the field. And know this – in every field there is, it is none but I who am the Knower of the Field; I am the soul in every body.'

'This body-field You talk about, Krishna,' interrupted Arjuna, 'is it my physical body?'

'It is, but it is also much more than that,' explained Krishna. 'Your physical body is made up of the same great elements – air, water, fire, earth and space – that make up the Universe; therefore, the elements are part of the body-field too. So are the five sense organs – the eyes, the ears, the tongue, the nose and the skin; and the five sensations they produce – sight, hearing, taste, smell, touch. The organs that help you learn and do things – the mouth that speaks, the arms that work, the legs that take you places, are in the field too.'

'And what of my mind, my intelligence, my thoughts? Are they the Knower of the Field?'

'Not quite,' said Krishna. 'That invisible something inside you that helps you think, act and feel is also part of the field itself. That "something" is made up of (1) your Intellect, which helps you think; (2) your Ego, your sense of "I", which makes you see yourself as separate from the world, saying "This body I see in the mirror is *me*, these things are *mine*", and makes you act accordingly; and (3) your Mind, that invisible, untouchable thing that makes you feel emotions – pain, pleasure, hate, desire.'

'If the Knower isn't the Intellect, or the Ego, or the Mind,' cut in Arjuna, as a sudden thought occurred to him, 'it has to be my Awareness, the core of my being, the part that knows and understands what is going on instinctively, without the help of the Mind or the Intellect.'

'Most people would agree with you,' said Krishna, 'but even your Awareness, or your Understanding, isn't the Knower. That is part of the field as well.'

Arjuna was puzzled. 'What else is left, Keshava? Who is the Knower?'

'The Knower, or the Atman, Kaunteya, is not your sense of "I", not your intelligence, not even your awareness. What is it, then? It is that which has no beginning and no end; that which sages describe as neither existent nor non-existent. With a million hands and feet, heads and faces, the Knower hears everything though he has no ears, sees everything though he has no eyes, knows everything though not through a small, limited mind. He dwells in the world but also surrounds it, he is not only inside every body but also outside every body, enveloping everything while permeating everything. He is light years away and yet beside you, he is still and yet constantly on the move. He is indivisible, but every creature and every tuft of grass contains a little piece of Him; He is the reason creatures are born, and the reason they die before He births them again.

'He is the Light of lights that lies beyond all darkness. He is the goal of all knowledge, and He is the knowledge that can get you to that goal.'

'But how do I get this knowledge, Keshava?' asked Arjuna. 'How can I know the Knower in me?'

'Be humble, Partha, be honest; do not hurt anyone, do not be deceitful, or pompous. Be patient, be pure in word and deed, have self-control, serve your teachers. Learn to enjoy the pleasure of your own company; keep away from the pointless chatter of the crowd. Watch the action on the field that is your body and mind – birth, death, joy, sorrow, pain, pleasure; participate wholeheartedly in this action, according to the role you have been given in this life – be mother or father, son or daughter, server or served, warrior or priest. But don't let any of it affect you. Think of Me constantly, with unswerving devotion and unwavering discipline. And then you will have true knowledge. For I say to you, anything but this true knowledge is non-knowledge – it is knowledge of the field, not of its Knower.

'Do not make the mistake of thinking that what the body feels is real, that what happens in the field is what matters. What is sown in a field is what is reaped; that is its nature. The Knower knows this truth, and is not disturbed. What the body experiences – disgust and desire, rage and sorrow, pain and pleasure – is the result of its interactions with the world through its senses, its limbs, its mind, its ego, its intellect and its awareness; that is its nature. The soul has nothing to do with it. The Knower knows this truth, and is not disturbed.'

What a state of grace that would be, marvelled Arjuna to himself, if one could only achieve it! What bliss to be able to watch everything that was happening to you like you would watch a piece of theatre, participating in it, being involved in it, laughing and weeping with the characters, but not being affected by the events on stage, never taking it personally, knowing it was only make-believe! He wondered if his soul would ever, *could* ever, get there.

'Men take different paths on their journey of self-discovery,' said Krishna, as if he had read Arjuna's mind. 'Some discover it through meditation, some by knowledge, and some simply by doing their work well and selflessly. Others, who don't know how to travel any of these paths, listen to the advice of their teachers and worship Me with devotion; they also succeed in their quest.

'Wise is the man who recognizes that the soul is not the body, for he knows that the soul remains unstained by the body's joys and sorrows, its anger and its hate, its virtues and its vices. Happy is he who realizes that his soul is no different from the Supreme Soul, who dwells in everything, never-perishing, everlasting, while the body is born a thousand times, and dies a thousand times. Know this, Partha, the Knower is only the Witness and the Sustainer. He makes the body's actions possible, he experiences everything the body experiences, but still remains separate, unaffected, unmoved.

'The truly wise see that the doer of all action – good or bad – is the body, not the soul. They know that the soul only stands witness to the actions of the body, and, therefore, remains faultless, however faulty the action. The soul has no qualities, Kaunteya – just like space, which is everywhere but is unaffected by all that happens in it and around it, it is untouched by the body's actions. The soul is the Lord of the field; it illuminates the field just as the one glorious sun illuminates the entire world.'

Lessons from the Gita

14. You are God. No, seriously.

क्षेत्रज्ञं चापि मां विद्धि सर्वक्षेत्रेषु भारत ।
क्षेत्रक्षेत्रज्ञयोर्ज्ञानं यत्तज्ज्ञानं मतं मम ॥१३-२॥

kshetragyam chaapi maam viddhi sarva-kshetreshu bhaarata
kshetra-kshetragya-yor-gyaanam yat-taj-gyaanam matam mama

Know me as the Knower of the field in all fields, O Bharata. The knowledge of the field and the knowledge of its knower is what I consider true knowledge. (13-2)

What is the Gita actually saying in this shloka? Essentially, that God Himself is the soul (Knower of the Field) of all beings (all fields), that there is really no difference between your soul and the soul of the Universe, or the Universal Soul.

Right at the beginning of this book, there is a Gita prayer shloka that everyone who wants to study the Gita recites before they begin reading. The prayer says that the Gita contains the essence of all the great wisdom of the Upanishads, which are ancient Sanskrit texts that the Hindus believe were divine revelations. One of the Mahavakyas, or Grand Pronouncements, of the Upanishads has just three words – *Tat Tvam Asi*; You Are That. The 'You' in the statement refers to whoever is being spoken to, the 'That' refers to the Supreme Soul. There is no room for misunderstanding here, or conflicting opinions. The statement is as straightforward and as unequivocal as it can get – You Are That; You Are The Supreme Soul. It is this great wisdom that the Gita reiterates in this shloka.

But how can a man – even if he is big and burly and seven feet tall – be the same as God, who contains universes within himself? How can God, who has 'the sun and moon as his eyes', fit into the limits of a human body? For the simple reason that we are no longer talking about the physical – how big something is, what it contains, what it looks like. We are talking about the basic core essence of something once the physical is stripped away.

For instance, if someone said a light bulb was actually no different from a treadmill, you would recommend that he get himself to a doctor pronto. But that is because you are thinking of the physical characteristics of each – a light bulb is small, gives off light that helps you see in the dark, shatters when it is dropped, and so on, while a treadmill is huge, is a good way to get exercise while watching TV, is usually used as a towel stand at home, and so on.

Now let's say we stripped away the physical and got to the essence of the two objects in our example. We would instantly see that the essence of both, the 'life force' of both – the reason why a light bulb shines and a treadmill functions – are the same, and its name is electricity. Similarly, a notebook is the same as a dining table, for they are both essentially wood; a brick wall is the same as a china teacup, for they are both essentially mud; a blonde, blue-eyed cheerleader is the same as a hippopotamus wallowing in an African swamp, for they are both essentially bones and muscles, or, if you break it down further, because they are both essentially carbon, hydrogen, nitrogen, oxygen, phosphorus and sulphur.

And it is in that sense that the 'You Are God' statement works. From the 'You', strip away the physical body, the mind, the senses, the ego and the awareness, leaving just your essence, the life force that makes you possible. From the Universe around you, strip away everything that can be seen, heard, smelt, tasted, touched, understood, felt and imagined. Yes, that means even 'space', a concept which you *can* imagine, is gone. What is left is 'That', the essence of the Universe, the life force that makes the Universe possible, which is often called God. And because 'That' is the life force of the Universe and everything in it, and you are part of the Universe, it stands to reason that the universal life force is the same as your life force.

Ergo, you are essentially the same as God. *Tat Tvam Asi*. You Are That.

Or if you want to get all poetic and olde-worlde about it, Thou Art That.

Believe it!

Not this, not this

How do you define something that is by its very nature indefinable? How do you describe something that is not like anything you have seen, heard, smelt, tasted, touched, felt, thought about, or even imagined? How do you explain the concept of God, aka Supreme Soul, aka Brahman? The authors of the Vedas, the ancient Hindu texts, struggled with that one for a long time.

Usually, when we describe something to someone who hasn't seen it, we rely on comparisons to other familiar things to build a picture in our listener's mind. 'Fuchsia is a deep pink,' we might say, 'mixed with the tiniest bit of purple.' Or 'Eating a *rasgulla* is like eating a sweet, milky sponge' or 'Neymar's game is a lot like Pele's'. But when our mind cannot come up with a suitable comparison immediately, we use another technique – negation. We describe something not by explaining what it *is*, but what it is *not*. Like, 'That fabric is a little rough, but not as rough as khadi, and not even as rough as raw silk, or even linen; but it isn't as soft as cotton either – I'd put its texture somewhere between cotton and linen.' Gives a pretty decent picture of the feel of the fabric, right? And you haven't even described what it is.

The Vedic scholars also found the negation technique useful to describe God, who in their opinion was the Indescribable, Incomparable and Unimaginable One. They called this technique *Neti, Neti* – Not this, Not this (or 'Neither this, nor that'). He is not earth, they said, nor fire, wind, water or space. He is not what you see or hear. He is not what you can imagine. He is not pain, He is not pleasure; He is neither wholly inside you nor wholly outside you. And so on. They also described the soul this way – it is not the senses, not the mind, not the intellect, not awareness. And so on.

The good part about this negation technique is that, whatever it may look and feel like at first, it is not taking

you further away from the truth; in fact, it is doing the exact opposite. Every time you figure out what something is not, you can cross that one off your list of possibilities. As your list gets shorter and shorter, you get closer and closer to nailing what it really is. As we saw for ourselves in our 'rough fabric' example.

It is sort of like how doctors work, or detectives — they get to the truth (What is causing the headache? Who committed the crime?) by a process of elimination. Getting to the bottom of the truth about God is much, much harder, but the process is the same.

१४

the yoga of the differentiation of the three modes
―――◄◄◄►►►――― gunatraya vibhaga yoga

IN WHICH KRISHNA PROVIDES US WITH THE PERFECT EXCUSE FOR ALL OUR FAULTS – 'IT'S NOT ME, IT'S MY NATURE!'

Arjuna was still, taking in every word that Krishna had told him. It was all a bit overwhelming. New, unfamiliar ideas jostled around in his head, but strangely enough, they had the effect of clearing his mind rather than clouding it. He supposed that was what happened when your interlocutor was God Himself. Krishna looked at him, his eyes shining. 'Understand this, Kaunteya,' he said. 'I am the Knower in all fields, but I am also their origin. My womb is Prakriti, Mother Nature, who is constantly changing, following the cycle of birth, life and death like clockwork. Into her I, Purusha the Knower, cast my seed as Supreme Father and step back to watch the play unfold. Every form of being, born of every kind of womb, springs from that union.'

'And that's how it happens,' Arjuna said, his face alight. 'That's how a bit of You finds itself into all of us.'

Krishna nodded. 'Our essence is the same, Arjuna. Your soul is as immortal and free as I am, and can remain unattached to Prakriti, the changing world around you, if it so wishes. But so charmed is your soul by Prakriti that it consciously chooses to play with her, through the senses, the body, the mind, the awareness and the intellect. Before you know it, you are bound to Prakriti by her twisted, three-stranded rope; you begin to believe that what happens in Prakriti unconsciously – birth, death, pain, pleasure, desire, anger – is real, that it is all done by *you*, felt by *you*, made to happen by *you*. Or that they are all happening *to* you. Both are not true.'

'A three-stranded rope?' Arjuna frowned. 'What do You mean, Lord?'

'Know this, Mahabahu,' said Krishna. 'Goodness (Sattva), Rajas (passion) and Tamas (dullness) are the three strands of Nature's rope, which bind down the soul. Rajas is part of Nature's creative side – birth, energy, movement, change, action, the season of spring. Tamas is part of Nature's destructive side – death, decay, inertia, heaviness, winter. Sattva is the state in between – harmony, wholesomeness, lucidity, stillness, summer.

'Of these, Sattva, pure and good, can illuminate your soul in its shining light, but even Sattva is a golden shackle. Once you enjoy that happy state of Sattva – good health, knowledge, harmony and peace – you get attached to it, not willing to let it go, yearning for it when it is gone, as it will.

'Rajas springs from desire, yearning, dissatisfaction with the way things are. It prompts you to action, and once you act, it attaches you to the result of your action, makes you want a particular outcome, makes you happy when you get it, unhappy when you don't. Beware, Kaunteya, for Rajas binds your soul tight.

'Tamas is born of ignorance – it confuses, deludes, makes you negligent. It binds your soul to indolence, sleep, sloth, laziness.

'The power of goodness makes slaves of the happy, makes them constantly hunger for peace and harmony. Passion enslaves the doers, traps them in an unending cycle of wanting something and then acting to get it. Dullness enslaves the careless and negligent, who never want to leave that torpid state of ignorance and lethargy.'

Too true, mused Arjuna. No wonder human life was so full of torment.

'Goodness, passion and dullness are present in all beings, Arjuna,' Krishna went on, 'combined in different ways, constantly in motion, rising and falling, one following the other. They are all present in you; they are *your* nature. Sometimes goodness prevails over the other two, making you feel calm, radiant, happy, at peace, fulfilled; sometimes passion prevails, making you feel restless, greedy, impatient, excited, excitable, full of energy. At other times, dullness prevails, which destroys clear thinking – anger, fear, grief, confusion arise in this state.

'From goodness is born knowledge, and the fruit of good action is joy; from passion arises greed, and the fruit of passionate action is pain; from dullness arises negligent and wrong action, and its fruit is ignorance.

'The man who strives to stay in the state of Sattva rises to higher rewards, while the man who dwells in Rajas remains trapped in the middle regions, and the man who is sunk in Tamas descends to the underworld. Also know this, Kurunandana – he who meets death in a Sattvik (*pronounced saa-tt-vik*) state of mind goes to the pure worlds of the saints, and is born again in a wise and righteous family. He who meets death in a Rajasik (*pronounced raa-ja-sik*) state is bound to be born again in a family of doers, bonded to action once again. And he who meets death in a Tamasik (*pronounced taa-ma-sik*) state, when he returns, will be born in the womb of a dull being that has neither knowledge nor wisdom.'

'So I must try my best to remain in the state of Sattva, mustn't I?' asked Arjuna.

'That's a start,' said Krishna. 'But the wise man realizes that there is something more joyous beyond all three modes of his nature, and strives for it. He understands

that it is these modes of his nature - and not he himself - that are the doers of all action; and thus he is freed from the pain of birth and death, and becomes immortal.'

'How will I know him, Lord, this man who has escaped Prakriti's three-stranded rope of Sattva, Rajas and Tamas?' asked Arjuna. 'What is his way of life?'

And the Blessed Lord replied. 'I have told you all this before, but I will again, O Pandava. This man feels no dislike for any of the three modes when they arise in him, nor does he long for any of them when they are replaced by another. He stands aside, watching, unconcerned, while goodness, passion and dullness rise and fall in him, each following each in turn. He treats blame and praise the same, considers friends and foes as equals, looks upon a piece of gold and a clod of earth with the same eye, feeling neither love for one nor hatred for another. He remains the same in both pleasant and unpleasant situations. And he serves Me unfailingly with devotion and with love.

'The soul of such a man, Arjuna, becomes one with Me - the home of the Supreme Soul, the home of absolute bliss.'

Lessons from the Gita

15. Your better nature is in there somewhere. Become best friends with it to avoid being reborn as a bandicoot.

Hindus believe that everything in Nature is in constant flux between three states of being, or Gunas, called Rajas, Sattva and Tamas, which broadly echo the natural cycle of Creation, Preservation and Destruction. That is why the holy Trinity of Hindu gods has one god representing each – Brahma the Creator, Vishnu the Preserver and Shiva the Destroyer. All three gods are equally revered, and all their roles are considered equally important. One of the ways in which Nature showcases the three Gunas is through the annual cycle of seasons – spring is the season of new birth or creation, when Nature comes into bud; summer is the season of long warm days, when Nature comes into fruit; and autumn and winter are the seasons when Nature goes into a long sleep, or death.

The same three states are part of human nature too. We are all of us different and unique because the three Gunas combine in each of us in different proportions to make us who we are. Sattva is linked with goodness, Rajas with passion, and Tamas with dullness and darkness. People who have a higher proportion of Sattva in their nature are more inclined towards seeing the bright side of things and radiate calm in every situation. They are seekers of knowledge, who enjoy living in the world of ideas, and prefer their own company to other people's. People with a higher proportion of Rajas in their nature are natural leaders – they are active, energetic, constantly setting goals for themselves and achieving them, passionately arguing for or against something, showing their friends that 'impossible is nothing'. Those in whom Tamas reigns are natural followers – loyal, patient, easy to work with, stable.

However, whether you are naturally a Sattvik, a Rajasik, or a Tamasik person, you will, like every other human, go through different states of being every day, depending on which Guna is dominating your mind at that time.

Sattva is the *I-feel-balanced* state. When Sattva dominates, you enjoy the activity you are engaged in, you can think clearly, and you are at peace – neither disturbed about something that's already happened nor anxious about something that is going to happen. It's a great state to be in, a state you should always try to get back to.

But too much Sattva is a problem. It could make you smug and complacent, even arrogant – you begin to diss others who are not as calm or happy, you begin to think that you are somehow cooler than everyone else. When something happens that shows you that you are really not as cool as you think, you lose your Sattvik state. Another problem could be that you get so attached to your happy state that you don't want to do anything else, even stuff that you should be doing to continue staying in that happy state.

Let's say you are listening to your favourite band on your headphones. You have a bowl of potato chips by your side, you're chatting with your friends over the Internet, and your parents are out to dinner. It's your perfect evening. You know that you are supposed to be working on a card for your friend's birthday tomorrow (in other words, you know you need to get out of Sattva and into Rajas), but you are so reluctant to switch off the music, or stop chatting that you don't end up doing it. The next day, you don't have a card for her, and she seems a little upset with you. That makes you really upset with yourself, not only because she is upset but because you know you could have made that card but didn't. Sattva goes out the window, Tamas comes in.

Rajas is the *I-feel-alive* state. When Rajas dominates, you feel full of energy, ready to take on the world. You feel life could not be better unless you make it so, and you are fully prepared to go out and do what it takes to make it happen. It's a good state to be in, because it occupies you completely. When you're busy doing something, there is no time to brood. When your mind is engaged in activity, there is no space for mean, dangerous or foolish thoughts. But too much Rajas — hyperactivity — is a problem. It heightens the emotions, making you aggressive, anxious and stressed. This in turn robs you of the power to think clearly, and the slide into Tamas begins.

Let's say that in our previous example, you had tons of homework to do that evening when your parents were out. Unlike a card for a friend's birthday, homework is not optional, so you decided to do it *while* listening to music and eating chips and chatting on Facebook. Your peaceful Sattvik state now turns into a Rajasik state.

You start off well, and you're just beginning to congratulate yourself on what a super multitasker you are, when all the distractions come together and ensure that you get a bunch of sums wrong. Now you have to cross them out and start over, which gets you all annoyed and/or depressed. Rajasik state goes out the window, Tamasik state comes in.

Tamas is the *I-feel-sluggish/upset* state. When Tamas dominates, you feel bored and lazy and lethargic, or unhappy, angry, sad, stressed, confused, or scared. In our example, in the first instance, you were angry with yourself for not making the birthday card. The right thing to do now would be to admit your mistake, apologize to your friend and make it up to her in some other way. Likelier than not, she will understand, you will be friends again, and you will return to your Sattvik state. But Tamas is clouding your mind now that you are upset. You are confused and unable to make the right decision. You tell her she is being immature, that birthday cards are for babies.

Obviously, she gets mad, and you feel even worse and go deeper into Tamas.

Let's go to the second instance, when you got stressed and depressed about having to do your sums over. The right thing to do in this situation would be to turn off the music, get off the Internet and start concentrating on your sums. But Tamas is clouding your mind, so you curse your teacher for giving you so much homework instead, and are all cranky with your parents when they return, blaming them for going out and enjoying themselves when poor you are at home alone struggling with homework. This pushes you further into Tamas. Not fun.

The thing to remember is that the Sattvik state — the balanced state — is always there inside us, waiting to be reclaimed whenever it slips away. It is up to us to reach for it, consciously, so that we can bring our lives back into balance. The more often you reach for it, the better you will get at finding it and yanking it to the surface.

There are simple ways to change your state of mind. If you are feeling depressed and sluggish and Tamasik, force yourself into a state of Rajas, i.e., do something — go for a run, call a friend, pull out your to-do list and finish a couple of tasks on it. You will feel energized, happy, and have a sense of accomplishment at the end of it. If you are feeling stressed from too much Rajasik activity, take a break. Sit down by yourself in a quiet place for 10 minutes, take a few deep breaths, and try and empty your mind of all thoughts. Or simply remove yourself from the scene of activity and sink into glorious Tamas – take a nap, flip channels on your TV, have a snack. It will help you recharge, and you will soon be ready for Rajas again. From Rajas to Sattva isn't a long journey – any activity that is right and unselfish and good naturally leads to Sattva.

You see why Sattva is a good state to aim for? Peace, contentment, the joy that comes from being and doing good – you'd have to be a special kind of silly not to want that. You also see why Tamas is not a great state to be in – the Gita says that anyone who is in that state when death comes will be 'reborn in the womb of a dull being', where 'dull being' is usually interpreted to mean some form of plant or animal life. And you don't really want to be reborn as a bandicoot now, do you?

SATTVIK   RAJASIK   TAMASIK

Meet the parents. . .er. . .parent

In this famous shloka, Krishna reveals that there is really no one else but Him who brings the Universe to life, for He is both mother *and* father to the Universe.

सर्वयोनिषु कौन्तेय मूर्तयः संभवन्ति याः ।
तासां ब्रह्म महद्योनिरहं बीजप्रदः पिता ॥ १४-४ ॥

sarvayonishu kaunteya moortayah
sambhavanti yaahaa
taasaam brahma mahad-yonir-aham
bijapradah pitaa

*Whatever forms are produced in whatever womb,
O Son of Kunti, they have all come from my womb,
which is the great womb of Nature, and I am the
Father who casts my seed into it. (14-4)*

१५

the yoga of the supreme person ----◀◀◀◆▶▶▶---
purushottama yoga

IN WHICH THE CONVERSATION TAKES AN UNUSUAL TURN – AND GOES TOPSY-TURVY

'The ancients speak of an imperishable tree – the sacred Ashvattha,' said the Blessed Lord. 'They say it is an upside-down tree, with its roots above and its branches below.'

Arjuna started, confused. Hadn't they just been speaking of the three-stranded rope of Prakriti that keeps the soul tied down, and the need to cut through it to free the soul? They were suddenly talking about trees now?

He opened his mouth to protest, then thought better of it. Before this morning, he would have done it without a second thought, and demanded that Krishna be more logical. But everything had changed since then. This was not his best friend Krishna speaking – well, it was and it wasn't, for, as Arjuna had just discovered, his best friend was also the dazzlingly beautiful, awe-inspiringly fearsome Supreme Being himself. No longer, decided Arjuna, did he have the privilege to interrupt, disagree with or debate anything He said. The most he would allow himself was to humbly and respectfully ask for a clarification, and that only when the Lord had finished speaking.

Also, so far at least, the Lord had proved to be a good and patient teacher. There was obviously a reason why he had brought up the tree at this point, and Arjuna knew he would benefit from behaving like a good student, and listening.

Casting his doubts from him, Arjuna leaned in to listen.

'The Ashvattha's roots, its real source, are in the heavens,' said Krishna. 'They originate from where everything in this Universe originates, they take birth in Me. As the tree grows down towards the earth, buds and shoots begin to sprout, for that is the nature of a tree. The shoots grow out and thicken, becoming branches that bear millions of leaves. Think of the Vedas, which carry the wisdom of the ages, as the leaves of this tree. It is I who nourish this tree; I am the sap that runs through its trunk and its branches, its tiniest leaf, strengthening it.

'As the branches get close to the earth, they plunge in, becoming roots. From these roots, new trees arise; a forest grows and sprawls around the primal tree, hiding it from view. To a dweller in this vast, endless forest, it seems as if the forest has sprung from the earth; it appears that it is the earth that sustains it. The only way for him to see the true picture is to hew down the forest with the sharpest axe he can find, trunk by trunk, until the forest is gone; only then will be revealed, in all its glory, the great trunk rising to the sky, the forest's true source of nourishment.'

Arjuna saw where this was leading. A thrill of anticipation ran through him. Krishna saw it, and smiled.

'The soul is like the Ashvattha, Partha. It has its roots in Me; it is nourished and sustained by Me. But Prakriti – with its twisted rope of goodness, passion and dullness – creates the branches of desire, from which sprout the shoots of action, which give rise to desire once again, in an endless cycle. Very soon, the branches have grown thick and hard. They put down roots, and become giant trees themselves. The soul forgets its heavenly birth, its divine origins. It begins to believe that it is the forest that sustains it. It ignores the leaves of wisdom and chases after the fragrant flowers that are everywhere in bloom, and the luscious fruit hanging from the boughs – it makes gathering them its goal.

'But fruits rot, and flowers wither, causing the gatherer grief and pain. The forest, and everything in it, changes constantly, and dies a thousand times. Nothing is permanent in this forest of illusions except the one true trunk that rises to the sky; nothing is permanent, nothing is *real*, in this world except your soul, which has its roots in Me.

'And that is why I say to you, Kaunteya, hew down the deep-rooted forest of desire, anger, selfish action, greed, pain and pleasure within you with the sharp axe of detachment. Raze it to the ground so that the wisdoms of the original leaves stand revealed, so that your soul may see where it really comes from, and who sustains it. Take refuge in Me – the Unchanging, the source of all energy, all life. For I will give you everlasting joy – why waste time chasing after anything less?'

Arjuna bowed. His faith in Krishna the teacher had not been unfounded.

'Let Me reveal to you, Arjuna, what really happens to your immortal soul, which is but a fragment of my own self, when it comes into contact with the world. There is an instant, overwhelming attraction

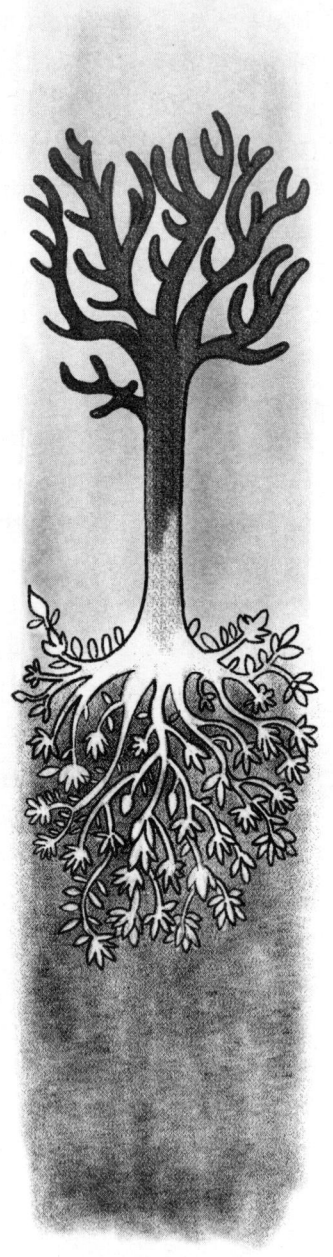

between the two, and the soul is sorely tempted to enjoy the beauty of the world. So it draws to itself the five sense organs, through which it can experience the world, and a sixth sense, the mind, which can hold all its desires. But it is still not complete – how can it really interact with the world if it does not have a physical body?

'And so the soul – along with the six senses it has gathered – takes up residence in a physical body. It enjoys the experiences its sense organs bring to it, and the thoughts and emotions flowing through its mind. When the body dies, the soul leaves, taking its six senses with it, and finds another physical body to inhabit, for it still has unfulfilled desires. And so it goes, over and over. The soul, bound to desire, and therefore bound to suffering, chases after pleasures that do not last, endures pain it could have avoided, lives a life it need not live.'

I suppose we've always known it, thought Arjuna to himself, stunned. We have always known how pointless it is to chase after ephemera, things that do not last. We've always known that real happiness lies somewhere beyond the material. And yet, and yet, we never stop chasing. He shook his head, marvelling at human foolishness.

'The wise know this,' Krishna said, 'they see the truth. They see that the soul, the spark, the life force in every being – whether it is the splendour in the sun and the moon, the nourishing sap in plants, the fire in the gut of every living creature that, fanned by its breath, converts food into vital energy – is really Me, the giver of everlasting joy. The others, deluded by the forest of desire, miss seeing Me completely.

'Listen well, Bharata, for I will now reveal to you a secret, sacred wisdom. The man who knows Me as the Foremost Among Beings, the Supreme Reality, the Unchanging Lord who is everywhere and in everything, the Sustainer of all the Worlds – he is truly wise. Such a man has all the knowledge that there is to be had. He adores Me with all his heart, and thus his life is fulfilled.'

Give us this day our daily digestion

अहं वैश्वानरो भूत्वा प्राणिनां देहमाश्रितः ।
प्राणापानसमायुक्तः पचाम्यन्नं चतुर्विधम् ॥१५-१४॥

aham vaishvaanaro bhootvaa praaninaam
deham-aashritaha
praanaa-paana-samaayuktaha pachaamy-annam
chaturvidham

In the bodies of all beings, I become Vaishvanara, the fire of life. Mingling with the two breaths, I digest the four kinds of food. (15-14)

In most cultures, and across religions, thanks are given to God before a meal for the food on the table. Hindus have many such prayers too. One of them is this shloka above, which Hindus chant to pray for good digestion.

So what is this Vaishvanara, then? Let's see.

In this chapter, Krishna says that he is the splendour of the sun and the moon, and the life-giving sap in plants. All three of these are connected. We know, through what we have studied in Science class, that sunlight helps green plants convert carbon dioxide and water into oxygen and sugars (stored as sap in plant stems and leaves, and as sugars and starches in fruits and vegetables). Science also tells us that without plant sugars, neither herbivorous nor carnivorous animals would survive, since neither group has the ability to manufacture its own food.

The Gita says the same thing, except that it calls sunlight, moonlight (which ancient Hindus believed enhanced the nutritional value of plants) and plant sap 'Krishna', and says that nothing could survive without Him.

Now, how do creatures like us – living beings that are not plants – convert the many kinds of food we eat – cola, chips, rice, roti, samosas, ice cream and birthday cake, for instance – into vital energy for our bodies? Simple, says the Gita. It is done by Krishna again, when he becomes the miraculous Vaishvanara, the fire of digestion, in all our bodies. Fanned by two 'winds' – one which pushes the food towards the stomach and the other which pushes undigested food out – Vaishvanara helps us digest 'four kinds of food' and converts all of it into the energy we need to live and work.

Krishna, therefore, says the Gita, is the producer of the food (sunlight), distributor of the food (plant sap), and consumer of the food (Vaishvanara).

But surely there are more than *four* kinds of food? Not really. When the Gita mentions four types of food, it means (1) Food that you chew (rice, samosas), (2) food that you drink (cola, lassi, litchi juice), (3) food that you suck (the pulp from mangoes, boiled sweets) and (4) foods that you lick (pickles, ice cream in a cone). That pretty much covers it, right?

What is common to the Ashvattha and Jack's Beanstalk?

They both connect earth to sky! And it isn't just them — there are dozens of such 'connectors' across cultures and religions around the world. Most stories of these connectors place them at a location that (in Latin) is called the Axis Mundi, the centre of the world, the point where the four cardinal directions meet. It is from and through the Axis Mundi (AM) that prayers and other communications are sent out to higher worlds, and blessings come down to lower worlds to be shared with all humanity.

You already know of one of the Hindu Axes Mundi ((the plural of Axis Mundi is Axes Mundi, not Axis Mundis) — the sacred fig tree or the Ashvattha, from the banyan family. FYI, the Ashvattha is also called the peepul tree, sacred to Hindus; or Bodhi tree, sacred to Buddhists; or *Ficus religiosa*, sacred, as all trees are, to botanists — and you can guess why they named the species that.

Here are other popular AM symbols, both from Indian and other world cultures.

Mountains – Since they are so hard to climb and since their peaks seem to touch the very sky, mountains, particularly snow-covered ones, are very popular as AMs. In Hindu mythology, we have Mount Kailash, the home of Lord Shiva, and Mount Meru, the sacred mountain that was used as the churn for the great Churning of the Ocean. Other mountain AMs include Mount Fuji – sacred to the Japanese, Mount Zion – sacred to the ancient Hebrews, Uluru or Ayer's Rock – sacred to the Pitjantjatjara people of central Australia, and Mount Olympus, abode of the gods in Greek mythology.

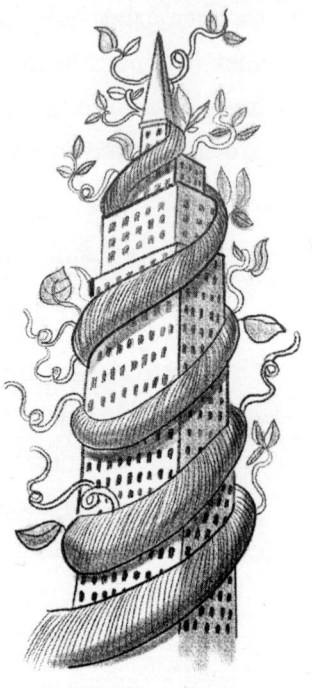

Trees – Trees are often used as symbols of the AM because they display the entire cycle of creation – birth, growth, fruition and death – on an annual basis. The Tree of the Knowledge of Good and Evil in Paradise, which Adam and Eve were forbidden to eat from, and did, causing God to evict them from the Garden of Eden, is an AM symbol. So is Yggdrasil, the world tree from Norse mythology, which connects the heavens to the underworld, and under which Odin, father of the Norse gods, received enlightenment. Believe it or not, the Christmas tree is an AM too, from well before Christianity was born! As is Jack's Beanstalk, the magical climber that connects two worlds.

Man-made structures – Sometimes, people built structures to mimic mountains and new AMs were created – the Pyramids of Egypt, for example, or the ziggurats of the ancient Mesopotamians, which had temples on top. Tall towers have been used too – the Tower of Babel and Jacob's Ladder in the Old Testament (they are both great stories – look them up!) are as much AMs as the Eiffel Tower in Paris or the Empire State Building in New York City (ever wonder why Rick Riordan put the gods of Olympus on this particular building? Now you know!). In fact, the ziggurat-like *gopurams* that sit atop south Indian Hindu temples, the rounded *shikhara* towers of north Indian Hindu temples, the tall domes of Buddhist stupas, the minarets of mosques and the spires of cathedrals are also AMs. Even a rocket ready for take-off could be seen as an AM symbol – after all, this one, when launched, will actually connect the earth to other realms!

१६

the yoga of the distinction between the divine and demonic endowments ····◄◄◄◆►►►···· daiva asura sampada vibhaga yoga

IN WHICH KRISHNA RECOMMENDS THAT YOU KEEP YOUR DEMONS LOCKED UP – OR ELSE

'Two kinds of beings inhabit this world, Partha,' said the Blessed Lord. 'One kind lets his divine side rule his mind, the other lets loose the demons in his nature.'

Arjuna nodded. He had always suspected it – that people were all essentially the same, neither innately good not inherently evil, or, to put it another way, *both* innately good and inherently evil. The difference between people was the choices they made. The difference was which side of their nature people allowed to take charge of their heads and hearts.

'What are the qualities of the divine-natured man?' Krishna said. 'Fearlessness is one, whether in the face of opposition, adversity or death. So is a pure mind, great self-control, a sense of sacrifice and the ability to practise charity in the right spirit. He stays on the path of goodness, this man, following the teachings of his teachers and the scriptures. He speaks the truth, forgives easily, and is free from anger, violence, greed, malice and excessive pride. This man of courage and vigour refrains from finding fault in others. He is gentle, modest, and compassionate to every other being.

'The demonic-natured man, Kaunteya, is the exact opposite. He is conceited and arrogant, showy and ostentatious, harsh, cruel and given to frequent and ruthless anger. Good conduct is not for him, for he does not know the difference between good and evil; nor is the right way of living, for he cannot tell what is right and what is wrong. He knows not the meaning of sacrifice and renunciation; he preaches one thing and practises another.

'Such men are ruled by ignorance; they do not see that this Universe functions according to moral laws, that there is a pattern of cause and effect, that actions have consequences; they believe that the world runs on desire alone, that the fulfilment of those desires is the path to happiness. They cast the scriptures aside, and deny My existence, believing that there is nothing beyond the world they experience through their senses.'

A vision rose in Arjuna's mind of the palace at Hastinapura. In the centre of the vast gambling hall, he saw his strong, brave brothers, their heads bowed, their spirits defeated. His gut twisting, he saw Prince Dushasana drag his beloved Draupadi by her hair into the packed hall. He heard her scream, plead, beg for mercy, curse her powerless husbands, while he sat, paralysed. And above her screams, he heard Duryodhana's malevolent laughter rolling over the heads of his brothers, crashing into his brain . . .

A red mist began to rise in front of Arjuna's eyes. Instantly, he clenched his teeth, shook it away, determined to remain in his Sattvik state. Calm flooded his being. He gathered his senses and focused them on Krishna.

'Reeling under this false belief,' Krishna went on, 'these lost souls of little understanding exercise no self-control; they give themselves up to never-ending desire, and are forever agitated – full of fear that their desires will not be fulfilled, full of anger when they are opposed, and full of anxiety, once the desire is fulfilled, that they will lose what they have. Their actions are selfish, their intents impure – they strive to gather to themselves vast hoards of wealth, by unjust means, believing that this is everything.'

'Puffed up with arrogance, full of ignorance, they say to themselves, "This I wanted, and this I now have. Now I want that; I will own it tomorrow, come what may. These riches, these things, are now mine, and I shall make sure I have more tomorrow." And they say, "This man is my enemy, he stands in the way of what I want; he needs to be eliminated. Tomorrow someone else will stand in my way, and him I will eliminate too. I am the only lord, there is no other. I am successful, mighty, rich, high-born, I have no equal. I will perform all the rituals

I am supposed to, I will practise charity to earn some goodwill for myself, and I will be fine. I will make merry, for that is what life is about; there is nothing else."

'But such men, Partha, are bewildered by their own thoughts, entangled helplessly in the web of their own ignorance. They enjoy no peace. Addicted to the fulfilment of desire, they fall into a foul hell of their own making, the purgatory of their own minds.

'Drunk on power and wealth, they perform extravagant sacrifices that are meant only to glorify themselves. Intoxicated by their own glory, these malicious men despise their fellow creatures, and so despise Me, the constant, watchful dweller in every being.

'Know this, Arjuna. These malignant haters of men, these despicable creatures who loathe Me and deny Me in themselves and in others, I hurl them back again and again into unworthy wombs, as demonic as themselves, so that they never escape the cycle of births and deaths, so that they are forced to live another life, and another, and another, in abject misery and anxiety, never knowing peace, never knowing true happiness, never attaining Me.'

Arjuna shuddered. There was not a hint of anger or agitation in the Lord's voice; He had spoken of the terrible punishment that He would hand out to demonic men in his usual straightforward manner, His tone calm and matter-of-fact. Somehow, thought Arjuna, that made the whole thing even scarier.

But the Blessed Lord was speaking again.

'Fear not, noble Pandava,' he said, and his voice was full of compassion, 'for you possess the qualities of the divine-natured. The diabolic men shall not escape the bondage to the cycle of births and deaths, but the divine-natured will be freed from it forever.'

Arjuna bowed low, his heart overflowing with gratitude. The Lord had said that he was divine-natured, and he accepted it with joy. But he wasn't sure how it had happened. What had he done right, he wondered, what pitfalls had he unknowingly sidestepped? How had he ensured that his divine nature had triumphed? As always, Krishna read his mind.

'There are three gates that lead to hell, to unrelenting darkness, and their names are Desire, Anger and Greed. Avoid opening them, Kaunteya, and the demons stay inside. The man who knows the scriptures knows this; he does what is good for his soul, and so he comes to Me.

'But the man who casts aside the wisdom of the scriptures, whose actions are guided only by his desires, he descends to the darkest realms, attaining neither happiness nor perfection; he does not come to Me.

'And therefore I say to you, Partha, pay attention to the words of the scriptures, the holy books, the texts that hold the wisdom of the ages; let them guide your actions. Let them help you decide what action is right and what is wrong. Do your work in this world according to their rules, and you will be free.'

Lessons from the Gita

16. There is an easy-peasy way to stay out of hell. Just avoid the paths marked Desire, Anger and Greed.

This lesson is all that a good lesson should be – it's succinct (you only need to remember three words), clear (we all understand what desire, anger and greed are) and simple to follow. Well, in theory, at any rate.

The problem is that the three paths are so devious. You have thought about each of these paths, you have resolved to avoid them, you actually believe you have the self-control and the willpower (or the won't-power, if you like) not to go anywhere near them, and then, suddenly, BAM! You're *on* one of them. The part where you look at the path-marker, realize it is a forbidden path and decide not to go down it? That hasn't even happened! Somehow, the path itself has snuck up on you, from behind, and now you're on your way to hell.

The three paths also sort of lead naturally from one to the other. Desire comes first, always. You see a lovely dress in a shop window, the latest model of the iPhone, the cool sneakers your favourite sports company has just launched – and you want them for yourself. You wish you could be part of one particular gang in school, you wish that quiet, nerdy girl in class would be your friend.

Desire is insidious – one minute you are walking along whistling a merry tune, with not a care in the world, and the next you are in agony, wanting something so bad that your very life seems empty and completely worthless without it. Desire is agony. Unfulfilled desire is a worse kind of agony.

Hot on desire's heels comes anger — at yourself for already having spent your birthday money on another dress; at your penny-pinching parents who believe that since you have a perfectly good phone already, you have absolutely no need for another; and at sports gear manufacturers for pricing shoes so high. You are angry with everyone in the gang you wish you could be part of, because they haven't invited you in, and angry with everyone in your own gang, for not being cool enough.

Anger is lacerating, all-consuming. It slams into you when you're least expecting it, going from 0 to 90 in a millisecond, destroying rational thought and the ability to make good choices — which, if you think about it, is really one of the most important qualities that separate us from the beasts. When you act in anger, it is almost certain you will regret your action, *even when your anger is justified*. Always better to wait for the rage to pass and then think calmly about the best course of action to take.

Anger is the worst kind of nightmare. When it explodes, it not only wrecks friendships and relationships — there is no way to take back hurtful, unwise things you said and did in anger – but also damages the angry person herself.

Greed – that ravenous, insatiable monster – is the third path. It leads on, once again, from desire. Once a desire has been fulfilled, the senses get to work again, shooting information to the mind about things beautiful to the eye, harmonious to the ear, soft to the touch, delicious to the tongue. The din of Greed's chant 'I want, I want' fills your mind, drowning out everything else. It brings in its wake envy and jealousy of anyone who has more, disdain for everyone who has less, and excessive pride in your own self. It makes you a miser – you cannot bear to part with what you have, and you live in constant fear that what you have will be taken away.

If that potent mix of negative emotions – Desire, Anger, Greed – jostling for space in your head isn't hell, what is?

HELL   HEAVEN

Angels and demons

द्वौ भूतसर्गौ लोकऽस्मिन्दैव आसुर एव च ।
दैवो विस्तरशः प्रोक्त आसुरं पार्थ मे शृणु ॥१६-६॥

dvau bhootasargau lokesmin-daiva aasura eva cha
daivo vistarashah prokta aasuram paartha mey shrinu

*In this world, two types of beings have been created –
the divine and the demonic. The divine I have already
described. Hear now, Partha, about the demonic. (16-6)*

Hindus believe that the demigods (Devas), and the demons (Asuras), are not very different from each other. They are really half-brothers, born of different mothers but sharing the same father, Prajapati. What makes a Deva a Deva is not his birth, but his noble nature, and what makes an Asura an Asura, again, is not birth but his dark nature.

It is important for Devas to *remain* good and noble if they want to continue enjoying the pleasures of heaven. If they don't do what it takes to stay on the good side, bad things can happen. Sometimes the Devas let their pride get the better of them, and have to suffer the consequences of their actions (they are cursed by sages and saints). Equally, it is possible for the Asuras to achieve great rewards. When they let their better natures come to the fore, they get to enjoy the consequences of those actions (they are given boons by the gods).

The same rules apply on earth. People who are usually divine-natured could cross over briefly to the other side when they allow anger or greed to rise in them. Usually-demonic men could cross over to the divine side when they keep their evil natures under control. Both groups will have to bear the consequences of their actions. Whether the consequences are good or bad will depend on the choices each made.

Back to the future

त्रिविधं नरकस्येदं द्वारं नाशनमात्मनः ।
कामः क्रोधस्तथा लोभस्तस्मादेतत्त्रयं त्यजेत् ॥१६-२१॥

trividham narakasyedam dvaaram naashanam-aatmanaha
kaamah krodhastathaa lobhas-tasmaad-etat-trayam tyajet

Three gates of hell lead to the soul's destruction, and they are Desire, Anger and Greed, Therefore, abandon these three. (16-21)

The Hindu heaven (Swarga) and hell (Naraka) are somewhat like the heaven and hell of other religions, with some important differences. Here are three of them.

1. In Hindu thought, there is a hierarchy of heavens and hells. There are lower heavens that are easier to reach by the good, and upper heavens that are a lot harder to get to. Then there are different hells – some texts put the total at 28 – for different sins.

2. Whether your soul gets sent to heaven or hell after your death, it will eventually be evicted from there and sent back to earth to live through another life. To Hindus, being sent to hell does not mean eternal damnation. In fact, it is a dry-cleaning service for the soul. First, the soul's sins are burnt off in the purifying fire. Then it returns, scrubbed clean, to the earth, to take on another human body. Hindus who have been good enjoy the pleasures of heaven for as long as the funds in their Karma (good action) bank hold out, but they have to return to the earth too, once the funds are gone.

3. To Hindus, being reborn on earth to live through another human lifetime is a punishment of the worst sort. The aim of every Hindu is to escape the cycle of birth and death, and become truly liberated from bondage. In other words, a Hindu's dearest wish is to go beyond the highest heaven to where the Supreme Soul lives, so that they can

become absorbed into the essence of the Lord and never return.

A little more about the 'returning to earth' bit. According to the Hindus, it is not God, sitting in judgment and weighing up your good deeds and bad deeds, who decides whether you come back to live another life or not, it is *your own soul* which does. If, when you die, your soul still has some unfulfilled desires that are connected with the world – 'I wish I had worked harder, I wish I had married the girl of my dreams, I wish I had been richer, I wish I had been a celebrity, I wish I had been kinder' – you will return.

The trouble with this, though, is that in your new life, even if you fulfil the desires of your previous one, you will end up accumulating new ones, and will be forced to return again. The only way to escape is to not play the desire game at all – if you leave this world with a mind and heart that is free of any desire, well, you will be completely and utterly free, and will never need to return again.

You see? You make your own destiny, really.

१७

the yoga of the threefold division of faith
shraddhatraya vibhaga yoga

IN WHICH KRISHNA HOLDS FORTH ON A VARIETY OF SUBJECTS – IN TRIPLICATE

'I hear what You say, Krishna,' said Arjuna, his brow furrowed in thought, 'but I have a question. What if someone has no access to the scriptures at all? What if he has never read them, what if he does not *know* how to? How can he follow the word of the scriptures then, as You recommend? What if he just follows his instinct, does what he believes is good and true, and worships You in the best way he knows, with a heart full of faith? What would You refer to such a man as? Would You call him Sattvik, a person of goodness? Would You call him Rajasik, a person full of passion and action? Or would You call him a dull, ignorant Tamasik?'

'It would all depend, Arjuna,' said the Blessed Lord, 'on the kind of faith this man practises. I call them good men – Sattvik – who worship the gods for their own sakes, seeking nothing but their blessings, taking joy in the act of faith itself. I call them passionate - Rajasik - who see the gods as givers of power and wealth, and worship them with great faith, seeking those very gifts from them. These men practise faith that is full of desire and greed. I call them ignorant - Tamasik -who make gods of ghosts and spirits, faithfully worshipping them. These men practise a dull faith, stained dark with ignorance.

'Those men who commit acts of violence on their bodies – piercing it with needles, denying themselves food and water, confusing self-torture with faith and devotion – they are truly misguided. This is not self-control, this is wilful harm and utter disrespect to the elements in their bodies that sustain them, and to Me, for I dwell in every body. This I consider demonic behaviour, this I do not appreciate.

'But it isn't just the texture of his faith that makes a man Sattvik, Rajasik or Tamasik. It is also his attitude to offering his actions to God, his attitude to penance and his attitude to charity. Why, even the food that he enjoys marks him out as one of the three.'

'The Sattvik man enjoys foods that are sweet, fresh, nourishing, juicy and agreeable to the system, for they fill his body and mind with energy, strength, health and joy. The Rajasik man enjoys foods that are bitter, sour, salty, spicy, pungent, exciting to the tongue but disagreeable to the system, for they cause pain, bad health, and irritation of the body and the mind. The Tamasik man takes a perverse pleasure in food that is tasteless, rotten, stale and impure – he is a scavenger, who eats the leftovers of others.'

Arjuna nodded. This part was easy enough to understand. He suspected the others would be more complex. But he had to know. 'What about the different textures of offering, Krishna?'

Krishna gazed indulgently at his eager student. 'Listen, Partha, and I will tell you.

'He who offers his every action up to the Universe, without expecting anything in return; he who believes that his every action is his sacred duty and therefore does not seek any reward for it; he who performs action that is completely unselfish and not for his own gain – his offering I call Sattvik.

'He who carries out every action with an eye on what he will gain for himself from it, who performs actions to gain admiration and appreciation from others, or as a display of his own power or wealth – his offering I call Rajasik.

'And he, Bharata, who does not think about his actions before doing them, who does not care how his actions affect himself or other people, who does not heed the words of the wise nor the rules of law and only acts according to the instincts of his animal nature, his offering is empty of faith; I call his offering Tamasik.'

'And what of the different textures of penance, Vasudeva?' asked Arjuna. 'Tell me about austerity and control, of the mind and the body and the wayward tongue. Tell me about the kind of penance the Sattvik man practises, for I would like to practise it too.'

'Understand, Partha, that there are three kinds of penances – the penance of the body, the penance of speech and the penance of the mind.

'To bow down before the gods, your teachers, the earth and its creatures, and wise people of every colour; to be pure and clean internally – by feeding your body the right foods – and externally – by being a stickler for personal hygiene and the cleanliness of your surroundings; to maintain the right posture always; to have control over the senses – this is the penance of the body.

'To speak words that do not hurt or harm; to only speak the truth; to engage in conversation that is both pleasant and beneficial to the listener; to repeat often the wise words of the scriptures – this is the penance of speech.

'To stay calm and composed in every circumstance; to only allow good and gentle thoughts to stream through your mind; to sometimes empty your mind of all thought and let silence reign; to be able to control your mind and prevent it from leaping constantly from one thought to another – this is the penance of the mind.'

They were all difficult, mused Arjuna, all three kinds of penances. But the penance of the mind was surely the hardest of all. 'And is he Sattvik who practises all three?' he asked.

The Blessed Lord shook his head. 'There are Rajasik and Tamasik men who practise all three too,' he said.

'What sets the three apart are their *reasons* for practising these penances.

'When this three-fold penance – of body, speech and mind – is done not to gain anything except a better understanding of oneself; when it is done only for the highest goal, which is to connect with one's own soul; when it is practised with a balanced mind and with complete faith in its wisdom, I call that penance a good penance, a Sattvik penance.

'When this three-fold penance is performed for worldly rewards – whether it is to gain other people's respect and admiration, or to win power and wealth for oneself – I call that penance the penance of desire, a Rajasik penance. The hard-won rewards from such a penance are temporary and unstable; they do not last.

'When this penance includes bodily harm and self-torture and it is performed stubbornly, with no clear thought, paying no heed to the voice of reason, in pursuit of a foolish goal that will eventually cause harm to others and to oneself, I call that penance the penance of darkness, a Tamasik penance.'

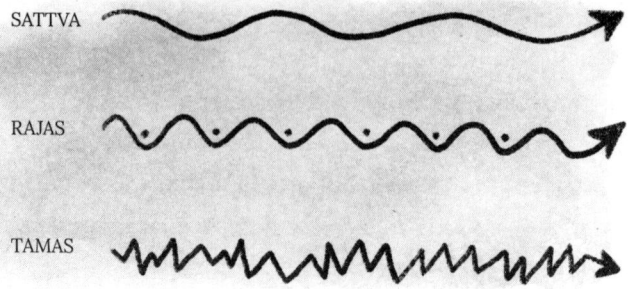

That wasn't as complicated as I had expected, thought Arjuna to himself, pleased. Or maybe he was simply getting the hang of this. Either way, he could feel the mists in his head clearing, feel the swirling thoughts slow down and begin to settle.

'And finally,' said Krishna, 'to the business of giving. Charity that is practised out of a sense of duty – simply because one feels it is the right thing to do – to a worthy person, at an appropriate time, with no expectation of reward or return from the recipient, is Sattvik charity.

'But charity that is practised reluctantly, or with the hope of some kind of return or some future reward, or as a repayment for past favours, that is Rajasik charity.

'And charity which humiliates the recipient, which is unsuitable or is laced with contempt, or charity which is practised towards an unworthy person, at an inappropriate time, that I declare to be Tamasik charity.'

Arjuna sighed. Too many men he knew belonged, sadly, to the third category.

'Chanting the sacred mantra "*Om Tat Sat*" – *The Supreme Is The Only Truth* – the wise and the good carry out their actions, offerings, penances and charity, with a faith that is steadfast and unwavering, and with no expectation of reward. Any offering given, any penance performed, any charity practised, *without* this kind of faith, Partha, is Asat, an illusion, a complete falsehood, and as far from Sat – the Real, the Good, everything I stand for – as can be. Such actions bring no rewards to the doer – neither on this earth nor elsewhere.'

Lessons from the Gita

17. You are what you eat. Or, as computer scientists might put it, 'Garbage in, garbage out'.

You already know this, of course, but the fact that an ancient book of wisdom also says so should make you pause and consider this undeniable fact once again – what you put into your body affects your mind, your actions, your energy levels, and most importantly, how you feel about yourself.

It is interesting that while most of us are pretty concerned about what we put *on* our bodies – how we dress, how we wear our hair, how we smell – very few of us really think about what we put *in* our bodies. And yet, most adult diseases – and juvenile versions of adult diseases – are very often directly related to the latter. Even if we put aside talk of disease for the moment, what about the big 21st-century problem called childhood/juvenile obesity? Or tooth decay? Both are proven beyond doubt to be almost always directly related to what we put into our bodies.

Let's say you have neither of these problems. You still know for a fact that after a truckload of junk food, your stomach craves for a hot, fresh, nutritious meal. When you have eaten out for too many days in a row – when you are on vacation, for instance – it feels wonderful to come back to a simple, home-cooked meal. Homesickness (which is a state of mind) when you are in boarding school, is very often closely connected with missing home food (which is a bodily need).

You only need to look at the diets of top sportspersons all over the world to know that they have one thing in common — they watch what they eat. They avoid oily, greasy, spicy, sugar-laden, over-salted and processed food like the plague, stocking up instead on fresh fruit and vegetables, lean meat, nuts, milk and eggs. They do not smoke or do drugs; they take alcohol almost entirely out of their diets. They do this not only because it keeps their bodies fit, but also because it is only when their bodies feel good that their minds can stay clear — to make split-second decisions about which shot to use, to focus only on the next lap, to come back from what seems like certain defeat to snatch the advantage once

again. Every sportsperson knows that her game on a given day will only be as good as she is feeling that day, and one of the basic ways to ensure that she is feeling good is to make sure her body is giving her no trouble.

Now let's expand the scope of our topic a little, and change 'You are what you eat' to 'You are what you consume', and you will see that it still holds very true. What do you 'consume' on a daily basis? The books, magazines and newspapers you read, the television you watch, the websites you visit, the social media sites you hang out on, the conversations you are part of, the music you listen to – all these are part of what you consume each day. Just like with food, there is good information you can consume – nourishing books, uplifting music, inspiring television programmes, and so on; there is stuff that is neither too bad nor too good; and there is absolute junk. Whether you like it or not, what you consume affects your mind, your mood and your actions.

Of course that doesn't mean you stop watching violent action movies altogether. Or that you never read a trashy novel that has nothing to recommend it except cheesy dialogue. All you need to do is to make sure that you also regularly include in your 'diet' a feel-good movie that celebrates the human spirit, or a television show about Science or Nature or History, or a book that makes you think and question, or inspires you, or fills you with peace, or hope, or laughter.

A truly balanced 'menu' would also include being part of warm and loving conversations with friends and family, and spending quality time with the one you love best – yourself.

Basically, fight the urge to reach for the junk food, both real and metaphorical. Be very picky about what you eat and drink and 'consume', even if it doesn't always make for the funnest meal. Do this, and you will stay in the pink of physical, mental, emotional and spiritual health always. Think it's worth a try?

A healthy mind in a healthy body

आयुःसत्त्वबलारोग्यसुखप्रीतिविवर्धनाः।
रस्याः स्निग्धाः स्थिरा हृद्या आहाराः सात्त्विकप्रियाः ॥१७-८॥

Aayuh-sattva-balaarogya-sukha-preeti-
vivirdhanaahaa
rasyaah snigdhaah sthiraa hridyaa aahaaraah
saattvika-priyaahaa

Foods that bestow long life, a stable mind, strength, health, happiness and joy; those which are juicy and nourishing and soft and agreeable, are much loved by the 'good' people, the Sattviks. (17-8)

The traditional Indian system of medicine, Ayurveda, believes that treatment for any condition should treat not just the condition but the entire body, and the mind. This is why a typical Ayurvedic treatment will involve yoga (for regaining physical fitness and stimulating certain organs), meditation and breathing exercises (to calm the mind and free it from stress), massages (for physical well-being), a strict diet (consisting of easy-to-digest 'Sattvik' food), and finally, medication.

So, according to Ayurveda, which foods constitute the healthy, calming Sattvik diet recommended in this shloka?

1. Fruits of all types, especially those that are naturally sweet;
2. All vegetables, except onion and garlic;
3. Whole grains like barley, wheat and rice;
4. Beans like rajma and chana, and dals;
5. Plant-based oils like sunflower, groundnut and olive oil;
6. Nuts and seeds, especially almonds that have been soaked in water and peeled;
7. Natural raw sugar, molasses, honey (in a glass of warm water with the juice of half a lemon squeezed into it);
8. Milk, butter, curd and cottage cheese;
9. Sweet spices, like cinnamon, cardamom, mint, basil, turmeric, ginger, cumin and fennel; and

10. Food prepared with love, for which you thank the Universe, before eating.

Foods to be avoided in a Sattvik diet include meat, fish and eggs, any highly processed food, alcohol, tobacco, stimulants like coffee and cola, spicy foods, garlic, onion, stale food, fruit and vegetables that are no longer fresh and therefore have lost their 'juiciness', and what we call 'junk food'.

Yup, the verdict on junk food, even 2,500 years ago, was a big No-No. So there!

On either side of the chariot drawn by the four white horses, on whose mast the monkey flag fluttered so proudly, the soldiers of both armies grew ever more restive. The commanders on both sides grew anxious too – would this midfield conversation never end? The little tableau that had been playing out on the chariot in front of them hadn't changed much since the conches had been sounded at dawn, except that the hero did not look quite so despondent any more, and that somewhere along the way, he had fallen to his knees and into a pose of complete and utter adoration for the cowherd prince who had volunteered to be his charioteer.

More nerve-wracking than the mistimed conversation was an unnerving suspicion that both sides felt deep in their bones but did not acknowledge to each other because it seemed so fanciful – time seemed to have come to a complete standstill at Kurukshetra. If Surya, the sun god, had progressed but a few lengths across the sky, Grandsire Bhishma could have forced the start of war, insisted that the conversation be abandoned. But Surya seemed as paralysed by the unexpected turn of events below him as everyone else. The early morning shadows showed no signs of shortening; they stayed immobile; nailed, it seemed to the nervous watchers, to the very earth.

In the Throne Room at Hastinapura, sensing that the conversation was drawing to a close, Sanjaya's voice grew more animated. Hearing it, the blind king shivered involuntarily, shaken by the deep, dark certainty that the war that he could have prevented was almost upon them, and that it would bring nothing but the worst kind of tragedy upon his sons, his clan and the land. He wished he could tune out Sanjaya's voice, shut down his own mind, and rush into oblivion, screaming, but he could not – the conversation was too riveting, even though every word Krishna said, every truth he spoke, only further sealed his boys' fates.

His sightless eyes bright with a horrible fascination, Dhritarashtra leaned forward to listen.

२८

the yoga of release by renunciation ----◄◄◄◆▶▶▶----
moksha sanyasa yoga

IN WHICH ARJUNA ASKS HIS FINAL QUESTION

'I wish to know, O mighty-armed Lord,' said Arjuna, 'the difference between "renouncing" and "not being attached". Is *giving up* the world, *giving up* action, *giving up* relationships, the same thing as *not being attached* to the world, *not being attached* to action, and *not being attached* in relationships? They seem very similar, but are they the same? I beg You to enlighten me, Hrishikesha.'

Said the Blessed Lord, 'Some learned men say that to *give up* action means not doing any action at all – they say all actions are evil, since they are done out of desire for personal reward. Others do not agree – they say actions that involve sacrifice, penance and charity are not evil, but good, and must be carried out.

'Here's what I say, O Best of the Bharatas. This, O Foremost among Men, is my final verdict.

'While acts of sacrifice, penance and charity must be performed, they only become truly "good" when they are done without the doer wanting anything in return for them – not even praise, not even if that praise comes from his own mind, for himself.

'Apart from these, actions that one has to perform because it is their duty – as a student, as a parent, as a merchant – *have* to be done. Abandoning your duties is unacceptable – I consider this kind of *giving up* Tamasik; such neglect of duty is born of a dark, ignorant nature.

'Then there are men who give up any action that is distasteful to them, or which they fear will cause them physical pain. This kind of selfish *giving up* is Rajasik; it brings no rewards.'

Arjuna almost smiled. In typical fashion, Krishna was laying the rules of 'action' out, clearly and simply, leaving no wiggle room whatsoever for those who wanted to twist the rules to their own benefit. He could guess what was coming next, but he wanted to hear it spoken by the Lord himself.

Krishna obliged, instantly. 'But know this, Arjuna,' he said, 'he who performs all his duties simply because he believes they ought to be done, *giving up* attachment to the rewards of his actions, *giving up* his actions themselves to the Universe, his giving up I call true giving up; him I call a good man, a Sattvik man. He is neither attached to certain actions because they bring him pleasure nor repulsed by other actions because they are distasteful, or will cause him pain. This man has no doubts about what *giving up* means, and whether it is different from *not being attached* – to him, both mean exactly the same thing.

'Those who do not practise this kind of giving up will reap the results of their actions after death, and those results could be pleasant, unpleasant, or both. But for those who practise giving up like the Sattvik man, there are no results to be reaped – these men escape the binding ropes of the world and become one with Me.'

IN WHICH ARJUNA LEARNS TO TELL NECTAR FROM POISON

Krishna paused to draw breath. Arjuna waited, eager to soak in every last bit of wisdom from a conversation that he realized was coming to an end.

'Now, Mahabahu,' went on Krishna, 'let Me tell you what all actions are born from. The five factors that make it possible for you to act, that urge you to act, and which determine what action you take, are these –

One: your body, for you could not act without your body;

Two: your sense organs and your limbs, which are the instruments that actually perform the action;

Three: your life force, which gives you the energy to act;

Four: your mind, or intelligence, or what you call "I", which processes everything your sense organs bring to it and decides what action to take; and

Five: the Universe, or fate, or your own past experience, call it what you will – which pushes you in a certain direction, makes you choose one action over another.

'No matter what action you do, in thought, word or deed, whether right or wrong, it is these five that are the "doers" of that action. Only a man of little understanding or great arrogance would imagine that there is only one doer, and that is himself, the factor we call "I".

'The man who understands the five doers, and knows that none of the five doers is the true him – he carries on his duties meticulously, without fear or desire, with an undisturbed mind. Such a warrior, even when he slays all his foes, does not in truth slay anyone, nor will he ever be forced to reap the results of his actions.

'What makes one act, Partha? Let Me break it down for you. First, there is an object, which is perceived by your sense organs and interpreted by your mind; second, there is your own "understanding" about that object, based on what you have heard, seen or experienced in the past, which makes you love it, hate it, or be indifferent to it; third, depending on your own feelings towards the object, you either choose to pursue it, reject it, or do nothing.

'Different people "understand" the same object in different ways. So what then is "true understanding", or "right knowledge"?'

Arjuna nodded. 'As You say, Lord, each person "understands" an object based on his own past experiences or his own limited knowledge, and therefore reacts differently to it. When that is the case, how can there be only one "right" way to react? What then is "true understanding" or "right knowledge"?'

'Listen, Kaunteya,' said Krishna, 'and I will tell you. Some people understand that even though there appear to be an infinite variety of creatures and objects in the world, they are all really the same below the surface. Such people do not differentiate between creatures, for they see beyond the external to the divine essence that is in all of them. This is right understanding, Sattvik knowledge.

'Some see the different creatures and objects in the world to be different and separate from each other, and separate from themselves. These men consider some creatures worthy of adoration, and others worthy only of spite; they love some objects and hate others; they think of themselves as superior to those they consider inferior. Such a skewed knowledge of the world is Rajasik knowledge.

'And then there are some who see only what they want to see and believe that what they see is the only thing that matters. They cling blindly to their narrow view and do not see the rest of the world at all or listen to any other opinion. This is truly a dull and ignorant kind of knowledge, a Tamasik knowledge.'

'I understand,' said Arjuna. 'Does it follow, then, that how a person *acts* in a particular situation, what he chooses to do, depends on how he *understands* what he sees, or the world?'

Krishna nodded.

'Sattvik action comes of Sattvik knowledge,' he said. 'The good man sees no difference between different creatures and therefore treats them all the same. He performs his duties – both pleasant and unpleasant – cheerfully, with energy and zeal, without being attached to them, and seeking no rewards.

'Rajasik action comes of Rajasik knowledge – the passionate man, concerned only with his own self, performs duties that he dislikes with reluctance, resisting and complaining; and those that he likes, or those that bring him some gain, with indecent eagerness.

'Tamasik action comes of Tamasik knowledge – the ignorant man, concerned neither with his own welfare nor the welfare of anyone else, and careless of the consequences of his action, does not even pause to reflect before he acts. He is unbalanced, stubborn, malicious, lazy, angry, sunk in gloom, and a procrastinator beyond compare.

'The Sattvik man, Partha, understands instinctively what ought to be done and what ought not to be done, what is to be feared and what not, and the difference between action and non-action. With steadfast mind, he controls his senses and his life-breaths. It is a difficult path he walks, this man, but the poison of pain and restraint that he drinks of turns eventually into golden nectar, and he achieves ultimate happiness.

'The Rajasik man is not always sure what is right and what is wrong; he often confuses the two because he is only concerned about how each action affects him. His steadfastness lies in holding on tight to things that give him pleasure – power and wealth, rich food and fine clothes. Such pleasures taste of nectar at first, but the happiness they bring is only fleeting, for the nectar soon grows mouldy and turns to poison, and causes him suffering.

'The Tamasik man, his mind dark with ignorance, is convinced about the rightness of wrongdoing, and sees everything from a twisted, perverted point of view. He steadfastly clings to his enemies – fear, grief, anger, arrogance, depression and sleep. This man is denied happiness, both lasting and fleeting – he does not know what lightness is, nor joy, nor cheer.'

IN WHICH ARJUNA LEARNS THAT HE MUST RESPOND WHEN NATURE CALLS

'You see, Parantapa,' said Krishna, 'how no creature on earth is free of the three binding ropes – Sattva, Rajas and Tamas – of its own nature? A person's nature influences how he thinks, what he does, how he sees the world, and everything else in between. No soul that has taken on a body can truly escape the dictates of its nature.'

It was a sobering thought. Arjuna wondered what his own nature was, and which of the three components of Prakriti dominated in him.

'According to their natures,' Krishna said, 'men are classified as Brahmin, Kshatriya, Vaishya and Shudra.

'He is called a Brahmin who is serene, who possesses great self-control and tolerance, who is pure and upright in action, thought and word, who is wise, and follows the teachings of the scriptures, even if he has never read them. His nature is dominated by Sattva.

'He is called a Kshatriya who is heroic in the face of adversity, a courageous warrior in the face of injustice, and generous to those who follow him. He is a resourceful and dependable leader, and will never turn his back on a righteous battle, or a mission he has undertaken. His nature is dominated by Rajas.

'He is a Vaishya who is involved in keeping the wheels of trade and agriculture moving, creating wealth so that society's every need is fulfilled.

'He is a Shudra who is happy to serve, diligent and loyal in the performance of his duty, content to follow orders and instructions, and to carry them out to the best of his ability.

'Listen well, Partha. It is only when a man does his own duty, devotedly and consistently, that he may hope to attain perfection. It is only by being true to his own nature, and by doing his own work diligently, that a man may truly worship God. Far better to follow one's own law even if one is not able to follow it to perfection, than to follow another's law, even if it is perfectly carried out. Far better to do the work suited to your nature, even if it is riddled with faults and errors, for what enterprise is not a process of trial and error? What work on earth is not clouded by defects, just as fire is invariably clouded by smoke?'

IN WHICH ARJUNA RECEIVES A PRECIOUS AND UNEXPECTED GIFT

Arjuna knelt before Krishna, his hands clasped in supplication. This was the wisdom of the ages, he marvelled to himself, complex philosophy handed down through generations of wise men, extraordinarily difficult for ordinary people to comprehend. But the way Krishna explained it, breaking it down into simple, precise, easy-to-digest chunks, made it a pure joy for the listener.

On his part, Krishna was well pleased with his earnest student, the mighty warrior whose very name struck terror in the hearts of his foes, and who knelt now with such disarming humility in front of him, drinking in his every word, unafraid to ask questions, unwilling to let a sentence pass without exploring its every nuance.

The conversation between the greatest teacher in the world and his most devoted student wound towards its climax, while the Universe held its breath and listened.

'Hear from Me, Kaunteya,' said Krishna, 'how a man can hope to attain perfection and become one with Me.

'He from whom desire has fled, who is not attached to anything or anyone around him, who has great self-control and is able to turn away from all the temptations offered up by the senses, whose understanding of the world is clear and unselfish, who is happy in his own company, who is moderate in what he eats, what he speaks and what he thinks, who meditates often and deeply on himself and the ways of the world, who has cast aside desire and anger, love and hate, arrogance and ego, and is always tranquil in mind – he is worthy of becoming one with Me.

'Fixing his thoughts on Me, surrendering all his actions to Me, taking refuge in Me, believing in Me, he crosses all obstacles by my grace, and reaches Me, the eternal place of rest.

'But if he is arrogant, if *you* are arrogant, and think to yourself, "I will not fight", your resolve will be in vain, trust Me, for your nature will compel you to do it anyway.'

Arjuna started, his senses suddenly on high alert. With marvellous felicity, Krishna had steered the discussion back to the battlefield, to him! His muscles tensing with anticipation, Arjuna focused on the Lord's next words as hard as he could.

'You are a warrior, Kaunteya; that is your nature. War is what you have been preparing for your whole life; it is pure conceit to think that you can will yourself not to be a warrior now.

'The divine force that lives in you, just as it lives in every other being, will turn you around like a puppet on a stick, and make you follow your nature – don't ever doubt that. Why do you fight it, Arjuna? Submit to the Lord inside you, the irresistible force of your nature, and do as it dictates.

'This is secret, sacred knowledge that I have revealed to you. Reflect on it, from every aspect, and then . . .'

Krishna paused in mid-sentence.

'And then?' prompted Arjuna, eager to receive the Lord's command, fully prepared to follow it to the letter.

'And then,' smiled Krishna, '*do as you choose.*'

The world stopped. Arjuna could not believe his ears. Even at this late stage in the Conversation, even after teaching him, with such patience, some of the greatest wisdoms in the world, even after revealing to him, in such glorious and terrifying detail, his true form, Krishna had not forced upon him any single course of action. *The Lord had still left the choice to him!*

His heart overflowing, Arjuna opened his mouth to speak, but Krishna had not finished.

IN WHICH THE WARRIOR RETURNS TO THE FIELD

'Listen again, one last time, to my supreme word,' said Krishna. 'You are beloved to Me, my dearest Arjuna, and that is why I persist, that is why I will tell you once again what is good for you. Simply fix your mind on Me, be devoted to Me, sacrifice everything to Me, surrender to Me, and thus you will come to Me. This I promise you, for you are so dear to Me. Do not fear, my friend, for I shall release you from all doubt, all grief.

'This wisdom that I have shared with you, this is precious, this is sacred, not meant to be repeated to anyone who is not moderate in his ways, who speaks ill of Me, who has no devotion in him, or who is not willing to listen. But teach this wisdom to My devotees, for no greater service to Me can any man do than spread My word and help his fellows to come to Me – I who am part of them.'

'And this I declare – he who meditates upon this conversation, *our* conversation, that man will have worshipped Me in spirit. Even he who merely listens to this conversation with faith, without scoffing, will be liberated, and join the ranks of the righteous.'

Arjuna trembled, completely overcome. Without wishing for it, without ever dreaming of such a wondrous, blessed thing, he had unwittingly become one half of what would be celebrated as one of the world's greatest conversations, a conversation that would be studied, debated, analysed, interpreted, taught and read over and over again through the millennia to come, by generations upon generations of both the wise and the worldly. It would bring, to its millions of readers and listeners yet unborn, joy and bliss, wisdom and reassurance, courage and solace. It would light their paths in this life and the several to come – a practical, compassionate and clear guide for negotiating the Kurukshetra that was the world, which was – he understood that now – nothing but the Kurukshetra that was the mind.

'O Partha,' said the Blessed Lord, and his voice was full of love, 'have you given my words your full attention? Have I succeeded, O Dhananjaya, in sweeping away your doubts and your worries, which were born of your ignorance?'

His eyes streaming, Arjuna fell to the ground, his body prostrate, his head at Krishna's feet.

'Destroyed are my doubts and gone my delusions, Achyuta!' he cried joyfully. 'Through your grace, wisdom is now mine. I stand firm with a mind clear of all conflict, my sweet Lord; I shall act according to your will.'

So saying, the greatest archer in the world mounted his chariot and drew himself up to his full height. Raising the mighty Gandiva to his shoulder, he surveyed the forces on either side with a dispassionate eye, feeling his adrenaline surge. As he gazed, the familiar faces blurred and merged – no longer did he see either side as friend or foe, brother or uncle, teacher or mentor; all he saw before him, clear as crystal, was his sacred duty, which was to lead his side to victory by doing his job as a warrior, and doing it well. It would be a terrible war, this one, but it had to be fought.

Arjuna raised his conch and blew with all his might. The earth shook, and both armies came to life, roaring with relief, thirsting for battle.

The warrior nodded to his charioteer. It was time.

Lessons from the Gita

18. (a) It is not your parents, or your work, that defines you. Your nature does.

(b) Stay true to your nature, and you will be happy.

Before we begin, a little refresher course about the Indian 'caste system', which you have probably studied about in History class.

Originally, the caste system was a way of classifying people according to their professions: the intellectuals – priests, scholars, teachers – were termed Brahmins; those who defended or administered the land – kings, the king's officers, soldiers – were termed Kshatriyas; those whose work revolved around money and entrepreneurship – moneylenders, traders, landowners, cattle-herders, shopkeepers – were termed Vaishyas; and those involved in manual labour – tailors, weavers, cobblers, butchers, cooks, sweepers . . . in short, anyone who served the other three castes – were termed Shudras.

If the caste system according to these original rules was still practised today, apart from the original traditional professions, several others would have been added on: Academicians, scientists, philosophers, economists, doctors, teachers, politicians, bureaucrats, activists, journalists, lawyers, venture capitalists, business barons, real estate developers, bankers, stockbrokers, airhostesses/stewards, valets, call-centre employees, tech-support staff, nurses, shop assistants, and more . . .

All four castes were considered equally important to keep society moving along smoothly, and no caste was therefore believed to be superior to any other. The analogy most often used to describe this is that the four castes are like four parts of the body. The head is the intellectual, thinking Brahmin, the arms are the doers of action – or the Kshatriyas, the stomach – which processes the body's food and converts it into fuel – is the Vaishya who creates wealth to keep the economy going, and the legs, which carry the body from place to place, are the Shudras who serve the other three castes. As you can see, no one part of the body is superior to any other – only when all the parts work together, doing their own duties diligently, can the body as a whole function with any efficiency.

But this is not how we understand the caste system any more. Somewhere along the way, a person's caste became linked to the family he was born into, not the profession he chose. If someone was born to Vaishya parents, for instance, he permanently became a Vaishya, never mind that he grew up and became a professor at Harvard or started his own political party. What was worse, some castes began to be considered superior to others, and the 'upper castes' began to believe that it was their right to treat the 'lower castes' badly.

In this chapter of the Gita, however, Krishna offers an alternative (and wonderful) view of caste. He declares that it is neither a person's profession, nor his birth, that makes him a Brahmin or a Shudra, but his *nature*.

High-thinking men and women (and boys and girls) who are calm and unruffled in every situation, who do not insist on only putting forward their opinions but are also willing to listen to others' points of view, who speak gently and little, who are tolerant and compassionate, who live a disciplined life – such people, according to the Gita, are Brahmins by nature. Yes, there is no age bar, or gender bar, or any bar at all!

In fact, Indian history has enough examples of these kinds of people – the saint Tukaram was a farmer, Kabir was born in a weaver's family, Mirabai was a princess, and Valmiki, the author of the Ramayana, was a reformed bandit, but they are all revered as saints of the highest order today because of what they had in common – their Brahminical (as defined by the Gita) nature. If you think about it, Mahatma Gandhi was both Brahmin and Kshatriya by nature, even though he was born in a Vaishya family.

Men and women who raise their voices against injustice, fight oppression and lead other men on heroic missions – against corruption, for instance, or garbage, nuclear warfare, or a bully in the playground – are Kshatriyas by nature. So are those who lead men on less noble missions – to wipe out an entire race, to assassinate a president, to bomb a village out of existence, to kill children.

Then there are people who are quick to spot good ideas and convert them into profit-making businesses. You probably know someone young who loves baking and sells his home-baked cupcakes at neighbourhood fêtes. Or organizes events – like birthday parties – for a fee. Or hires herself out as a DJ at college parties. Such entrepreneurs are Vaishya in nature.

And there are always plenty of people who neither want the responsibility of being in charge of anything nor the headaches of trying to create a business, but are very happy to follow instructions and do a good job of anything they are asked to do. You can spot them in every team in school – there is always someone who is a natural leader, who delegates tasks and makes decisions, and others who are natural followers, who take on the tasks they are given and do a great – or awful – job of them.

The thing to remember is this: a leader is not superior to anyone, just as a follower is not inferior to anyone. Each is just acting according to his or her nature. The Gita recommends this highly, in fact, saying that most progress – and most happiness – is achieved when people follow the dictates of their own natures and do what they do best, or what they are naturally inclined to do.

Let's say, for instance, that you stand for elections to the post of House Captain simply because you think it would be cool to be Captain or to beat your rival candidate. You know quite well that what you really enjoy is spending hours reading by yourself in the school library. What you do *not* enjoy is calling House meetings and writing reports, which is what a House Captain will be required to do. Now let's say you actually get elected. Very soon, you will be heartily sick of shouldering your responsibilities as House Captain. You will start shirking your duties and sneaking away to the library. Of course, such irresponsible behaviour will earn you no fans among your Housemates, and you yourself will feel awful about it. You have a complete lose-lose situation!

So before jumping into something, think about *why* you are doing it. When you feel bad that you did not get something you really wanted, ask yourself *why* you wanted it so badly, and whether the fact that you did not get it was not actually a good thing. The answers will help you decide whether or not you should continue with your action, or whether or not you should continue to feel bad.

If you are honest with yourself, you may often be surprised at your answers. Go on, try it and see!

EPILOGUE

The sound of Arjuna's conch shook the palace at Hastinapura to its rafters, casting everyone inside into severe panic. In the Throne Room, King Dhritarashtra sat as if frozen to his seat, his white-knuckled hands clutching its arms for dear life.

Beside him, in an uncharacteristic show of emotion, his charioteer wept openly with joy. It wasn't clear if the king was listening any more, but that did not stop Sanjaya from going on.

'Such was the blessed conversation between Vasudeva and the noble Partha,' he babbled incoherently, 'which has caused my very hair to stand on end. By the grace of the Sage Vyasa, who endowed me with mystic vision, I have had the rare and signal honour of listening to the supreme secret of life, taught by the master Yogi himself!

'O King! I am overcome with bliss! I thrill to the very roots of my being each time I recall this conversation, full of wondrous and sacred truths, between Keshava and Arjuna. I know it will always be this way.

'Ever and ever again I recall the wondrous form of Hari, which can never be explained but only experienced, and I am suffused, ever and ever again, with a joy not of this world, and my heart feels ready to burst.

'And this I know to be true, O King, and I am thus reassured – Wherever Krishna, the Lord of wisdom, stands shoulder to shoulder with Arjuna, the master of action, there, and there alone, will dwell forever, goodness and peace, prosperity and victory, and great, lasting glory.'

A matter of choice

In American author John Steinbeck's novel *East of Eden*, a Chinese American character called Lee gets obsessed with the Biblical story of the two brothers Cain and Abel, the sons of Adam and Eve. In the story, an insanely jealous Cain murders his brother, believing that God loves Abel more. For this sin, God casts Cain out of Eden forever. The two most accepted English translations (the original story is in Hebrew) of the conversation that God has with Cain about sin have God saying, either *'Thou shalt* rule over sin' (an assurance that Cain will eventually master his sinful nature) or *'Do thou* rule over sin' (an order to Cain that he must conquer his worse side).

Lee does not agree with either of these translations of the Hebrew word *'Timshel'*. He teaches himself Hebrew to understand the true meaning of the word, and becomes convinced, towards the end of the novel, that *Timshel* neither means 'Thou shalt' or 'Do thou' but *'Thou mayest'*. God, Lee believes, is giving Cain, and by extension, all humans, the *choice* to either resist wrongdoing – or plunge into it.

There is no such ambiguity in the Gita. The text has Krishna clearly giving Arjuna – and all of us – a similar power to choose the actions that we perform, the words that we speak, the thoughts that we think. Like every other great power, this one is as liberating as it is terrifying.

Terrifying because, well, there they go, all our excuses – 'I can't do the right thing because I'm too small / too weak / too insignificant / too poor / too tired to . . .' According to the Gita, there is no such thing as 'I can't'. What we're really saying is 'I won't'. Which means that all we need to do is to change the 'I won't' to 'I will' for the magic to begin to happen.

Yup, we have the power, but it comes with the responsibility of using that power well. In other words, (according to the Gita) it's we, and only we, who determine how we live our lives.

A last word about the Gitas

Wait, what? The *Gitas*? In plural? Uh-hunh. While the Bhagavad Gita is the first, the oldest and the most popular, there are several other Gitas around. There is the *Avadhuta Gita*, for one, in which the first guru, Dattatreya, sings (Gita literally means 'song') about the true nature of the world; as also the *Ashtavakra Gita*, in which the sage Ashtavakra reveals to Sita's father, King Janaka, the nature of the soul; the *Ganesha Gita*, sung by Ganesha; the *Ram Gita*, sung by Rama to Lakshmana; and the beautiful *Gita Govinda*, composed by the poet– saint Jayadeva, which celebrates the love of Krishna and Radha.

Interestingly, there are a couple of other Gitas that are part of the Mahabharata itself – like the *Anu Gita*, which is another conversation between Krishna and Arjuna, only it happens after the war; and the *Vyadha Gita*, where a butcher (yes, it isn't only gods and sages who are allowed to have their own Gitas) takes a hermit's ego down by telling him why his life, as a responsible householder, is just as spiritual a life as the hermit's. And there are at least a couple dozen more Gitas besides these.

Action with wisdom – an unbeatable combo

यत्र योगेश्वरः कृष्णो यत्र पार्थो धनुर्धरः
तत्र श्रीर्विजयो भूतिर्ध्रुवा नीतिर्मतिर्मम ॥१८-७८॥

yatra yogeshvarah krishno yatra paartho dhanurdharaha
tatra shreer-vijayo bhootir-dhruvaa neetir-matir-mama

Where there is Krishna, the Lord of yogas, and where there is Partha, wielder of the bow, there, in my opinion, is fortune, victory, prosperity and virtue. (18-78)

This is the very last shloka of the Bhagavad Gita – and one of the most unambiguous. It conclusively ends the argument on a number of questions, and on many levels.

First off, it sends out a strong and clear answer to King Dhritarashtra's first question, contained in the shloka that opens the Gita. 'Tell me, Sanjaya,' the king had asked, 'what is going on in that holy field of Kurukshetra, where my sons and the sons of my brother Pandu have gathered to fight?' If the king had hoped to hear that it looked as though the Kauravas were all set to win, since their numbers were so much larger, or even that the two sides looked evenly matched in skill and the result was difficult to call, Sanjaya's pronouncement in this shloka dashed that forlorn hope to the ground. What Sanjaya is essentially saying here, with no ambivalence whatsoever, is that the side that has Krishna and Arjuna in it is sure to bag victory.

Secondly, the Gita, in this shloka, declares that man's actions are incomplete and eventually 'unsuccessful' — both in terms of being right and in terms of bringing him lasting joy — if he does not work hand in hand with God, or if his action does not have God's blessings (this is a religious text we are talking about, after all!). If Arjuna is with Krishna, then victory and goodness and peace are guaranteed; if he chooses to work alone, thinking that he himself can make his actions bring him the results he wants, he is very sadly mistaken. All bets are off in this case, and there are no guarantees of lasting joy and peace.

There is a third way of looking at the message in this shloka. Krishna the Yogi is described here as the Lord of Wisdom, and Arjuna the warrior as the Master of Action. As you must have realized by now, Arjuna – the one asking all the questions, the one whose mind is conflicted with doubt, the one who is on the horns of a Really Big Dilemma – is really a metaphor for all of us.

We are all warriors in the daily battlefield of life, and we are often lost, full of conflict, doubt and fear, often ready to take action but rarely knowing what the right action is. What the Gita is saying in this shloka is that while Action is good, there is no way to ensure it is 'right' unless it is done hand in hand with Wisdom. Conversely, the Gita is also saying that Wisdom – knowing what the right thing to do is – is no good to you or anyone else unless you are also prepared to act on that knowledge. It is only when Arjuna is with Krishna, and Krishna is with Arjuna, that true 'victory', and right action, can result.

In one fell swoop, the Gita denounces both armchair philosophers, who think and talk, but do not 'act' nor practise what they preach, and reckless men of action, who do a lot, but don't quite think what they are doing through. It urges all of us to act, but act wisely; or, coming at it from the opposite direction, to reflect on what is right, and then go ahead and do it.

How can you ensure you are acting wisely? There is no easy answer to that one. But there are some hints, nudges and recommendations in the Gita, some starter-kit tips, as there are in every wise book, to help you along.

The rest, you will have to discover for yourself as you go along.

A NOTE FROM THE AUTHOR

Have you ever felt, at random points in your life, that you have been guided gently but firmly (read: dragged kicking and screaming) towards a path that wasn't ever on your radar of longing? And have you then, surrendering, walked that path, only to be overwhelmed with gratitude and awe for the blessings you begin to receive? I have.

It was my editor, mentor and friend, Vatsala Kaul Banerjee, who, close to a decade ago, first nudged me in the direction of the Bhagavad Gita, and then proceeded to urge me to undertake the task of retelling it for a young, 21st century audience. It was a formidable challenge, and one that I took my sweet time accepting, but when I finally began to read the original, aided by wonderful commentaries by philosophers, scholars, spiritualists and thinkers, both Indian and Western, I became so convinced that the Gita's wisdoms were of critical importance to the young that I was champing at the bit to begin. The process of writing itself, contrary to my expectations, was pure joy – I couldn't wait to be back at my desk each morning, to ruminate over the material I was tackling that day, before I set it down in writing. What Krishna was saying to his best friend, it seemed to me, was so clear, so wise, and so relevant, that my only responsibility was to make sure I didn't muddy up the messaging with jargon, overthinking, or messy writing. Not once in those days did I feel self-doubt or trepidation – that would come later, once the book was out in the world and in the hands of impressionable readers.

As it turned out, I needn't have worried. In the seven surreal years since the first edition of *The Gita for Children* came out, the book, having taken on a life of its own, has received more love than I imagined possible. As for me, I have travelled more miles and invested more man-hours talking about the Gita to audiences, young and old, across India and the world, than I have in any other 'project', apart from my children. Through the portal into ancient Indian philosophy that the Gita so graciously opened up to me, I have discovered other dazzling texts, interacted with and listened endlessly to spiritual masters, wonderful teachers and profound thinkers, written a 'prequel', *The Vedas and Upanishads for Children*, and begun the perspective-altering journey of learning the Sanskrit language for the first time.

If writing *The Gita for Children* was transformative for me, the effect the book has had on its readers has been nothing short of astounding. As of today, the book has sold over 100,000 copies, found its way into every continent on earth, and is now available in translation in four Indian languages – Kannada, Hindi, Telugu and Marathi, apart from Dutch. Three of those editions – Kannada, Telugu and Dutch – have come about through the unorthodox route of a reader loving the book so much that they have undertaken its translation of their own accord, and followed it up with the hard work of finding a publisher willing to buy the rights from the original publisher. In fact, the Kannada translation of the book was ready within a fortnight of the English version coming out, so inspired was the 74-year-old engineer-entrepreneur-writer who ordered one of the first copies of the book.

In the early days after the book's release, when it began to be clear that adult readers were enjoying the book (why were adults so drawn to a book that clearly declared that it was 'for children' and was only to be found in the children's section of bookstores? Perhaps because, as a wise old friend once hazarded, we are all children where the Gita is concerned), I despaired of it finding any traction with its intended audience. For one, it is a rare book that can speak to both adults and children in their respective registers. For another, a book of scripture isn't the first (or even the tenth) thing children would voluntarily pick up. I fretted that parents, seeing the book as 'worthy' or 'improving', would nag their children to read it, which, as we all know, is the best way to turn them against it.

But once again, my fears turned out to be groundless. Parents did not nag their children to read the book, they read it *with* them, and the Gita became part of dinnertime conversation in hundreds of homes. Many, many children who read it by themselves – the (few) eager readers coming to it without much urging, the more reluctant picking it up after hearing me talk about it at school or a children's literary festival – took the book and its lessons to their hearts. Perhaps the most gratifying message came from a social worker who introduced the book at a couple of juvenile shelters and remand homes that she was associated with, and wrote to tell me that the Gita's wisdoms had provided solace, and opportunities for reflection, to children there.

That this is so should come as no surprise to anyone, given that *The Gita for Children* is only a retelling of a compassionate, pragmatic, secular, non-judgmental text that has been revered in this land for millennia. What is deeply humbling is that, for reasons of its own, the universe chose me to be one among its countless interpreters. Writing a version of the Divine Song that is accessible to the young and vulnerable, from which they may draw strength, comfort and wisdom in times of distress and despair, has been one of the most rewarding experiences of my life. For this great opportunity, I shall forever remain immeasurably grateful.

Roopa Pai
Bengaluru, 2022

ACKNOWLEDGEMENTS

Until this book project came along, I had never engaged with the Gita in any but the most superficial manner. I took the challenge on with great trepidation, convinced I was the wrong person for the job. I was sure I wasn't even meant to understand complex metaphysics and philosophy, let alone be entrusted with the responsibility of interpreting it for a young, impressionable audience.

Over several months, as I read extensively and listened to several wise, lyrical, uplifting – and some completely bizarre – interpretations of the Immortal Conversation, I began to see just why so many people through so many generations had so many nice things to say about it. The experience was transformative on many levels, and although I can in no way claim to now fully 'understand' the Gita, I am deeply grateful to have had the opportunity to experience a first immersion.

I now believe that one arrives at the Gita – or any other book of wisdom – through a long and complex chain of choice and consequence; one doesn't simply wake up one morning and plunge into it willy-nilly. Several people helped me on my way to, and through, the Gita, and many thanks are due to them.

- To my friend and brilliant editor Vatsala Kaul Banerjee, who consistently steers my reluctant

chariot into vast, scary battlefields that I want to flee from, insisting gently but firmly that I fulfil my writerly Dharma.
- To my aunt-in-law, Tara Kini, for being so generous with her time, hugs, belly laughs and music, for living her life queen-size, and for sitting me down one afternoon last year, handing me three of her favourite commentaries on the Gita, and telling me, in her force-of-nature way, why I had to stop making excuses and take the challenge of writing this book head-on.
- To Sayan Mukherjee, who, to my great delight, got very excited on reading the first few chapters and agreed with alacrity to design the cover and populate the book with his evocative artwork.
- To the philosopher-president of India, Dr Sarvepalli Radhakrishnan, whose wise and scholarly commentary on the Gita became my first and most fundamental reference.
- To Dr Bibek Debroy (when he isn't being a busy, much-fêted economist and member of the NITI Aayog, Dr Debroy is an acclaimed Mahabharata expert), who read the completed manuscript in under two days and returned it not only with several valuable suggestions but also with an endorsement so unequivocal that I was finally reassured that it was safe to put the book out there.
- Ditto Anando Banerjee, voracious and catholic reader of books, including the Gita, who read the manuscript, loved it, and pointed out errors, besides

providing the title 'The Monkey Who Rode Shotgun' for a box he suggested I include. He also promised to buy many copies for all his son's friends once the book came out (there, Anando, it is in print – there's no backing out now).
- To Devdutt Pattanaik, whose counter-intuitive takes on our stories and their impact on our world view have served to alter mine – in the best way.
- To my children, Chetana and Rohan, who put up (with very bad grace) with a mum who, for several months, greeted them when they came home from school with unsolicited Gita gyana, conveyed in the breathless, bug-eyed fashion – do you see? do you get it? hanh? hanh? hanh? – of the newly proselytized.
- To my husband, Arun, who lives the word of the Gita without having read a single line of it.
- To Diana Broccardo and Mark Richards of Swift Press, UK, for taking this book to many more readers around the world.
- To the vast and inclusive ocean of notions that is India – I would choose you to be born in, in lifetime after lifetime.
- To the boundless wisdom, love, discontent, hope and unfulfilled promise we all hold within ourselves – seek and ye shall find.
- And lastly, to the eternal wisdoms of the Srimad Bhagavad Gita. Thank you for the music.

SELECT BIBLIOGRAPHY

I referred to and benefited from the wisdom of several books, websites, commentaries and people while researching this book. Some of the most remarkable insights and 'Aha' moments came through casual conversations with people familiar with the text, or books whose content was unrelated to the Gita except in a fundamental sense. The list below, therefore, is by no means a comprehensive bibliography. These are just the books and websites I read in their entirety, or those I found myself going back to most often.

Bhaktivedanta, A.C. and Swami Prabhupada: *Bhagavad-Gita As It Is*, Bhaktivedanta Book Trust, 1999.

Pattanaik, Devdutt: *Jaya*, Penguin Books India, 2010.

Easwaran, Eknath: *The Bhagavad Gita (Classics of Indian Spirituality)*, Nilgiri Press, 2007.

Isherwood, Christopher and Swami Prabhavananda: *Bhagavad-Gita: The Song of God*, Signet Classic, 2002.

Marballi, G.K.: 'A simple, modern translation and explanation of the Bhagavad Gita' accessed at www.journeygita.blogspot.com.

Prasad, Ramananda: *The Bhagavad-Gita for Children and Beginners*, International Gita Society, 2008.

Radhakrishnan, S: *The Bhagavadgita*, Harper Collins, 1993.

'Srimad Bhagavad Gita' accessed at www.bhagavad-gita.org

'The Bhagavad Gita with commentaries of Ramanuja, Madhava, Shankara and others' accessed at www.bhagavad-gita.us.

Visakha: *Our Most Dear Friend: Bhagavad-Gita for Children*, CreateSpace Publishing, 2013.